THE TOP Ninja Dual Zone Air Fryer Cookbook

1800 Days of Step-by-step Recipes to Master the Art of Healthy and Flavorful Cooking with Your Ninja Air Fryer

Jaymie C. Blank

Copyright © [2023-2024] by [Jaymie C. Blank]

All rights reserved.

This recipe book and its contents are protected by copyright law. The recipes, photographs, and words within these pages are the fruits of our passion for cooking. We kindly ask that you respect our creative efforts by refraining from reproducing, storing, or sharing any part of this book without our prior written consent.

Cooking is an art, and like any art form, it carries inherent risks. While we've strived to provide safe and accurate recipes, results may vary. We assume no liability for accidents, injuries, or allergies that may occur during cooking. Exercise caution, adhere to food safety guidelines, and consult experts when needed.

Thank you for choosing [Jaymie C. Blank]'s [The Top Ninja Dual Zone Air Fryer Cookbook]. Your support means the world to us, and we hope our recipes bring warmth and flavor to your culinary journey. By using this book, you agree to respect our copyright terms and understand our disclaimer.

Happy cooking

Sincerely,

[Jaymie C. Blank]

MAKE MEALTIME A CINCH WITH FULL-COLOUR PICTURES

GET THE MOST OUT OF YOUR NINJA AIR FRYER!

- Basic Information of Ninja Air Fryer

- Easy-to-Find Ingredients

- Step-By-Step Directions

- Quick & Flavorful Recipes

- Helpful Cooking Tips for Beginners and Advanced Users

CONTENTS

INTRODUCTION 5

Breakfast Recipes 7

Snacks And Appetizers Recipes 16

Vegetables And Sides Recipes 24

Beef, Pork, And Lamb Recipes 32

Poultry Recipes 41

Fish And Seafood Recipes 49

Desserts Recipes 57

How to Reduce Food Waste 66

Shopping Lists 67

Appendix A : Measurement Conversions 68

Appendix B : Recipes index 70

Fun In The Kitchen: 4 Kids-Friendly Air Fryer Recipes (+ Tips!) Let's step into the world of the Ninja Dual Zone Air Fryer, where delicious, crispy, healthy food is just a recipe away. With my guidance and the power of this remarkable device, your kitchen is about to become a culinary paradise full of flavor and creativity. Welcome to the Ninja Dual Zone Air Fryer Cookbook!

How does the Ninja Dual Zone Air Fryer work?

The Ninja Dual Zone Air Fryer is a cooking powerhouse that works by utilizing rapid hot air circulation and precise temperature control. Convection effect ensures even cooking and a pleasingly crispy texture, similar to deep-frying, but using far less oil. Whether you're air frying, baking, roasting or grilling, the Ninja Dual Zone Air Fryer offers a versatile, hassle-free solution for making mouthwatering meals.

1.Each basket is a bit smaller so things seem to cook faster, and get crispier than a larger space.

2.It seems to preheat a bit faster than the other, probably because there's a smaller space.

INTRODUCTION

3.I can cook two different things at different temperatures at the same time, so they're done simultaneously.

perfect when you want steak at two different "donenesses"

You don't have to clean out the initial pot to rotate in another dish after the first is done.

Hello fellow food lovers and culinary adventurers! My name is Jaymie C. Blank, and I'm thrilled to introduce you to a world of sizzling goodness and endless culinary possibilities. I believe the kitchen is the heart of every home, so I'm excited to take you on a delicious journey through The Ninja Dual Zone Air Fryer Cookbook. Within these pages, you'll find tons of recipes crafted for the Ninja Dual Zone Air Fryer. Whether you're a seasoned chef or just beginning your culinary journey, these step-by-step instructions and tantalizing flavors will captivate your taste buds and inspire your kitchen adventures. It's not just about preparing meals, it's about exploring the art of culinary magic and making delicious meals at the touch of a button.

Ninja Dual Zone Air Fryer Cookbook

Maximize the value of the Ninja Dual Zone Air Fryer

EXPLORING DUAL ZONES: With the Ninja Dual Zone Air Fryer, you have the exceptional opportunity to utilize two separate cooking zones. This opens up the world of simultaneous meal preparation, making it a practical choice for serving multiple courses or accommodating the varying preferences of your household.

UNLEASHING VERSATILITY: The true potential of your air fryer extends beyond air frying alone. Make the most of the included accessories like the cooking rack, crisper plate, and skewers to explore various cooking techniques.

OPTIMIZING TIME AND TEMPERATURE: Adjust temperature settings and timer durations according to the specific recipe you are preparing, and track the cooking progress closely to ensure that your dishes are cooked to perfection.

HARNESSING PREHEATING: Don't underestimate the importance of the preheat function. Preheating ensures that your air fryer reaches the desired cooking temperature before you begin.

HEALTH-CONSCIOUS COOKING: An air fryer is renowned for its ability to create crispy dishes with significantly less oil compared to traditional frying, helping you reduce calories and unhealthy fats while still achieving that coveted crunch.

EFFORTLESS CLEANUP: Keeping your air fryer in excellent condition is essential for its long-term performance. Make cleanup a breeze by ensuring that the cooking baskets and accessories are washed thoroughly after each use.

Breakfast Recipes

Biscuit Balls	13
Breakfast Casserole	12
Breakfast Cheese Sandwich	8
Breakfast Stuffed Peppers	10
Cinnamon Apple French Toast	13
Cinnamon-raisin Bagels Everything Bagels	11
Crispy Hash Browns	9
Donuts	8
Healthy Oatmeal Muffins	12
Honey Banana Oatmeal	11
Sausage & Butternut Squash	9
Spinach And Red Pepper Egg Cups With Coffee-glazed Canadian Bacon	10
Vanilla Strawberry Doughnuts	14
Yellow Potatoes With Eggs	14

Breakfast Recipes

Donuts

Servings: 6
Cooking Time: 15 Minutes

Ingredients:
- 1 cup granulated sugar
- 2 tablespoons ground cinnamon
- 1 can refrigerated flaky buttermilk biscuits
- ¼ cup unsalted butter, melted

Directions:
1. Combine the sugar and cinnamon in a small shallow bowl and set aside.
2. Remove the biscuits from the can and put them on a chopping board, separated. Cut holes in the center of each biscuit with a 1-inch round biscuit cutter (or a similarly sized bottle cap).
3. Place a crisper plate in each drawer. In each drawer, place 4 biscuits in a single layer. Insert the drawers into the unit.
4. Select zone 1, then AIR FRY, then set the temperature to 360 degrees F/ 180 degrees C with a 10-minute timer. To match zone 2 settings to zone 1, choose MATCH. To begin cooking, select START/STOP.
5. Remove the donuts from the drawers after the timer has finished.

Nutrition Info:
- (Per serving) Calories 223 | Fat 8g | Sodium 150mg | Carbs 40g | Fiber 1.4g | Sugar 34.2g | Protein 0.8g

Breakfast Cheese Sandwich

Servings: 2
Cooking Time: 8 Minutes

Ingredients:
- 4 bread slices
- 2 provolone cheese slice
- ¼ tsp dried basil
- 2 tbsp mayonnaise
- 2 Monterey jack cheese slice
- 2 cheddar cheese slice
- ¼ tsp dried oregano

Directions:
1. In a small bowl, mix mayonnaise, basil, and oregano.
2. Spread mayonnaise on one side of the two bread slices.
3. Top two bread slices with cheddar cheese, provolone cheese, Monterey jack cheese slice, and cover with remaining bread slices.
4. Insert a crisper plate in the Ninja Foodi air fryer baskets.
5. Place sandwiches in both baskets.
6. Select zone 1, then select "air fry" mode and set the temperature to 390 degrees F for 8 minutes. Press "match" to match zone 2 settings to zone 1. Press "start/stop" to begin. Turn halfway through.

Nutrition Info:
- (Per serving) Calories 421 | Fat 30.7g |Sodium 796mg | Carbs 13.9g | Fiber 0.5g | Sugar 2.2g | Protein 22.5g

Sausage & Butternut Squash

Servings: 2
Cooking Time: 20 Minutes

Ingredients:
- 450g butternut squash, diced
- 70g kielbasa, diced
- ¼ onion, diced
- ¼ tsp garlic powder
- ½ tbsp olive oil
- Pepper
- Salt

Directions:
1. In a bowl, toss butternut squash with garlic powder, oil, onion, kielbasa, pepper, and salt.
2. Insert a crisper plate in the Ninja Foodi air fryer baskets.
3. Add sausage and butternut squash mixture in both baskets.
4. Select zone 1, then select "air fry" mode and set the temperature to 375 degrees F for 20 minutes. Press "match" to match zone 2 settings to zone 1. Press "start/stop" to begin. Stir halfway through.

Nutrition Info:
- (Per serving) Calories 68 | Fat 3.6g |Sodium 81mg | Carbs 9.7g | Fiber 1.7g | Sugar 2.2g | Protein 0.9g

Crispy Hash Browns

Servings: 4
Cooking Time: 13 Minutes.

Ingredients:
- 3 russet potatoes
- ¼ cup chopped green peppers
- ¼ cup chopped red peppers
- ¼ cup chopped onions
- 2 garlic cloves chopped
- 1 teaspoon paprika
- Salt and black pepper, to taste
- 2 teaspoons olive oil

Directions:
1. Peel and grate all the potatoes with the help of a cheese grater.
2. Add potato shreds to a bowl filled with cold water and leave it soaked for 25 minutes.
3. Drain the water and place the potato shreds on a plate lined with a paper towel.
4. Transfer the shreds to a dry bowl and add olive oil, paprika, garlic, and black pepper.
5. Make four flat patties out of the potato mixture and place two into each of the crisper plate.
6. Return the crisper plate to the Ninja Foodi Dual Zone Air Fryer.
7. Choose the Air Fry mode for Zone 1 and set the temperature to 390 degrees F and set the time to 13 minutes.
8. Select the "MATCH" button to copy the settings for Zone 2.
9. Initiate cooking by pressing the START/STOP button.
10. Flip the potato hash browns once cooked halfway through, then resume cooking.
11. Once done, serve warm.

Nutrition Info:
- (Per serving) Calories 190 | Fat 18g |Sodium 150mg | Carbs 0.6g | Fiber 0.4g | Sugar 0.4g | Protein 7.2g

Ninja Dual Zone Air Fryer Cookbook

Spinach And Red Pepper Egg Cups With Coffee-glazed Canadian Bacon

Servings: 6
Cooking Time: 13 Minutes

Ingredients:
- FOR THE EGG CUPS
- 4 large eggs
- ¼ cup heavy (whipping) cream
- ¼ teaspoon kosher salt
- ¼ teaspoon freshly ground black pepper
- ½ cup roasted red peppers (about 1 whole pepper), drained and chopped
- ½ cup baby spinach, chopped
- FOR THE CANADIAN BACON
- ¼ cup brewed coffee
- 2 tablespoons maple syrup
- 1 tablespoon light brown sugar
- 6 slices Canadian bacon

Directions:
1. To prep the egg cups: In a medium bowl, whisk together the eggs and cream until well combined with a uniform, light color. Stir in the salt, black pepper, roasted red peppers, and spinach until combined.
2. Divide the egg mixture among 6 silicone muffin cups.
3. To prep the Canadian bacon: In a small bowl, whisk together the coffee, maple syrup, and brown sugar.
4. Using a basting brush, brush the glaze onto both sides of each slice of bacon.
5. To cook the egg cups and Canadian bacon: Install a crisper plate in each of the two baskets. Place the egg cups in the Zone 1 basket and insert the basket in the unit. Place the glazed bacon in the Zone 2 basket, making sure the slices don't overlap, and insert the basket in the unit. It is okay if the bacon overlaps a little bit.
6. Select Zone 1, select BAKE, set the temperature to 325°F, and set the time to 13 minutes.
7. Select Zone 2, select AIR FRY, set the temperature to 400°F, and set the time to 5 minutes. Select SMART FINISH.
8. Press START/PAUSE to begin cooking.
9. When the Zone 2 timer reads 2 minutes, press START/PAUSE. Remove the basket and use silicone-tipped tongs to flip the bacon. Reinsert the basket and press START/PAUSE to resume cooking.
10. When cooking is complete, serve the egg cups with the Canadian bacon.

Nutrition Info:
- (Per serving) Calories: 180; Total fat: 9.5g; Saturated fat: 4.5g; Carbohydrates: 9g; Fiber: 0g; Protein: 14g; Sodium: 688mg

Breakfast Stuffed Peppers

Servings: 4
Cooking Time: 13 Minutes

Ingredients:
- 2 capsicums, halved, seeds removed
- 4 eggs
- 1 teaspoon olive oil
- 1 pinch salt and pepper
- 1 pinch sriracha flakes

Directions:
1. Cut each capsicum in half and place two halves in each air fryer basket.
2. Crack one egg into each capsicum and top it with black pepper, salt, sriracha flakes and olive oil.
3. Return the air fryer basket 1 to Zone 1, and basket 2 to Zone 2 of the Ninja Foodi 2-Basket Air Fryer.
4. Choose the "Air Fry" mode for Zone 1 at 390 degrees F and 13 minutes of cooking time.
5. Select the "MATCH COOK" option to copy the settings for Zone 2.
6. Initiate cooking by pressing the START/PAUSE BUTTON.
7. Serve warm.

Nutrition Info:
- (Per serving) Calories 237 | Fat 19g | Sodium 518mg | Carbs 7g | Fiber 1.5g | Sugar 3.4g | Protein 12g

Cinnamon-raisin Bagels Everything Bagels

Servings: 4
Cooking Time: 14 Minutes

Ingredients:
- FOR THE BAGEL DOUGH
- 1 cup all-purpose flour, plus more for dusting
- 2 teaspoons baking powder
- 1 teaspoon kosher salt
- 1 cup reduced-fat plain Greek yogurt
- FOR THE CINNAMON-RAISIN BAGELS
- ¼ cup raisins
- ½ teaspoon ground cinnamon
- FOR THE EVERYTHING BAGELS
- ¼ teaspoon poppy seeds
- ¼ teaspoon sesame seeds
- ¼ teaspoon dried minced garlic
- ¼ teaspoon dried minced onion
- FOR THE EGG WASH
- 1 large egg
- 1 tablespoon water

Directions:
1. To prep the bagels: In a large bowl, combine the flour, baking powder, and salt. Stir in the yogurt to form a soft dough. Turn the dough out onto a lightly floured surface and knead five to six times, until it is smooth and elastic. Divide the dough in half.
2. Knead the raisins and cinnamon into one dough half. Leave the other dough half plain.
3. Divide both portions of dough in half to form a total of 4 balls of dough (2 cinnamon-raisin and 2 plain). Roll each ball of dough into a rope about 8 inches long. Shape each rope into a ring and pinch the ends to seal.
4. To prep the everything bagels: In a small bowl, mix together the poppy seeds, sesame seeds, garlic, and onion.
5. To prep the egg wash: In a second small bowl, beat together the egg and water. Brush the egg wash on top of each bagel.
6. Generously sprinkle the everything seasoning over the top of the 2 plain bagels.
7. To cook the bagels: Install a crisper plate in each of the two baskets. Place the cinnamon-raisin bagels in the Zone 1 basket and insert the basket in the unit. For best results, the bagels should not overlap in the basket. Place the everything bagels in the Zone 2 basket and insert the basket in the unit.
8. Select Zone 1, select AIR FRY, set the temperature to 325°F, and set the time to 14 minutes. Select MATCH COOK to match Zone 2 settings to Zone 1.
9. Press START/PAUSE to begin cooking.
10. When cooking is complete, use silicone-tipped tongs to transfer the bagels to a cutting board. Let cool for 2 to 3 minutes before cutting and serving.

Nutrition Info:
- (Per serving) Calories: 238; Total fat: 3g; Saturated fat: 1g; Carbohydrates: 43g; Fiber: 1.5g; Protein: 11g; Sodium: 321mg

Honey Banana Oatmeal

Servings: 4
Cooking Time: 8 Minutes

Ingredients:
- 2 eggs
- 2 tbsp honey
- 1 tsp vanilla
- 45g quick oats
- 73ml milk
- 30g Greek yoghurt
- 219g banana, mashed

Directions:
1. In a bowl, mix eggs, milk, yoghurt, honey, vanilla, oats, and mashed banana until well combined.
2. Pour batter into the four greased ramekins.
3. Insert a crisper plate in the Ninja Foodi air fryer baskets.
4. Place ramekins in both baskets.
5. Select zone 1 then select "air fry" mode and set the temperature to 390 degrees F for 8 minutes. Press "match" to match zone 2 settings to zone 1. Press "start/stop" to begin.

Nutrition Info:
- (Per serving) Calories 228 | Fat 4.6g | Sodium 42mg | Carbs 40.4g | Fiber 4.2g | Sugar 16.1g | Protein 7.7g

Breakfast Casserole

Servings: 4
Cooking Time: 10

Ingredients:
- 1 pound of beef sausage, grounded
- 1/4 cup diced white onion
- 1 diced green bell pepper
- 8 whole eggs, beaten
- ½ cup Colby jack cheese, shredded
- ¼ teaspoon of garlic salt
- Oil spray, for greasing

Directions:
1. Take a bowl and add ground sausage to it.
2. Add in the diced onions, bell peppers, eggs and whisk it well.
3. Then season it with garlic salt.
4. Spray both the baskets of the air fryer with oil spray.
5. Divide this mixture among the baskets; remember to remove the crisper plates.
6. Top the mixture with cheese.
7. Now, turn ON the Ninja Foodie 2-Basket Air Fryer zone 1 and select AIR FRY mode and set the time to 10 minutes at 390 degrees F.
8. Select the MATCH button for zone 2 baskets, and hit start.
9. Once the cooking cycle completes, take out, and serve.
10. Serve and enjoy.

Nutrition Info:
- (Per serving) Calories 699| Fat 59.1g | Sodium 1217 mg | Carbs 6.8g | Fiber 0.6g| Sugar 2.5g | Protein33.1 g

Healthy Oatmeal Muffins

Servings: 6
Cooking Time: 17 Minutes

Ingredients:
- 1 egg
- ¼ tsp ground ginger
- 1 tsp ground cinnamon
- ½ tsp baking soda
- ½ tsp baking powder
- 55g brown sugar
- ½ tsp vanilla
- 2 tbsp butter, melted
- 125g applesauce
- 61ml milk
- 68gm whole wheat flour
- 100gm quick oats
- Pinch of salt

Directions:
1. In a mixing bowl, mix together all dry the ingredients.
2. In a separate bowl, add the remaining ingredients and mix well.
3. Add the dry ingredients mixture into the wet mixture and mix until well combined.
4. Pour the batter into the silicone muffin moulds.
5. Insert a crisper plate in the Ninja Foodi air fryer baskets.
6. Place muffin moulds in both baskets.
7. Select zone 1 then select "bake" mode and set the temperature to 390 degrees F for 17 minutes. Press "start/stop" to begin.

Nutrition Info:
- (Per serving) Calories 173 | Fat 5.8g |Sodium 177mg | Carbs 26.6g | Fiber 2.1g | Sugar 8.7g | Protein 4.2g

Cinnamon Apple French Toast

Servings: 8
Cooking Time: 10 Minutes

Ingredients:
- 1 egg, lightly beaten
- 4 bread slices
- 1 tbsp cinnamon
- 15ml milk
- 23ml maple syrup
- 45 ml applesauce

Directions:
1. In a bowl, whisk egg, milk, cinnamon, applesauce, and maple syrup.
2. Insert a crisper plate in the Ninja Foodi air fryer baskets.
3. Dip each slice in egg mixture and place in both baskets.
4. Select zone 1 then select "air fry" mode and set the temperature to 355 degrees F for 10 minutes. Press "match" to match zone 2 settings to zone 1. Press "start/stop" to begin.

Nutrition Info:
- (Per serving) Calories 64 | Fat 1.5g | Sodium 79mg | Carbs 10.8g | Fiber 1.3g | Sugar 4.8g | Protein 2.3g

Biscuit Balls

Servings: 6
Cooking Time: 18 Minutes.

Ingredients:
- 1 tablespoon butter
- 2 eggs, beaten
- ¼ teaspoon pepper
- 1 can (10.2-oz) Pillsbury Buttermilk biscuits
- 2 ounces cheddar cheese, diced into ten cubes
- Cooking spray
- Egg Wash
- 1 egg
- 1 tablespoon water

Directions:
1. Place a suitable non-stick skillet over medium-high heat and cook the bacon until crispy, then place it on a plate lined with a paper towel.
2. Melt butter in the same skillet over medium heat. Beat eggs with pepper in a bowl and pour them into the skillet.
3. Stir cook for 5 minutes, then remove it from the heat.
4. Add bacon and mix well.
5. Divide the dough into 5 biscuits and slice each into 2 layers.
6. Press each biscuit into 4-inch round.
7. Add a tablespoon of the egg mixture at the center of each round and top it with a piece of cheese.
8. Carefully fold the biscuit dough around the filling and pinch the edges to seal.
9. Whisk egg with water in a small bowl and brush the egg wash over the biscuits.
10. Place half of the biscuit bombs in each of the crisper plate and spray them with cooking oil.
11. Return the crisper plate to the Ninja Foodi Dual Zone Air Fryer.
12. Choose the Air Fry mode for Zone 1 and set the temperature to 375 degrees F and the time to 14 minutes.
13. Select the "MATCH" button to copy the settings for Zone 2.
14. Initiate cooking by pressing the START/STOP button.
15. Flip the egg bombs when cooked halfway through, then resume cooking.
16. Serve warm.

Nutrition Info:
- (Per serving) Calories 102 | Fat 7.6g | Sodium 545mg | Carbs 1.5g | Fiber 0.4g | Sugar 0.7g | Protein 7.1g

Vanilla Strawberry Doughnuts

Servings: 8
Cooking Time: 15 Minutes

Ingredients:
- 1 egg
- ½ cup strawberries, diced
- 80ml cup milk
- 1 tsp cinnamon
- 1 tsp baking soda
- 136g all-purpose flour
- 2 tsp vanilla
- 2 tbsp butter, melted
- 73g sugar
- ½ tsp salt

Directions:
1. In a bowl, mix flour, cinnamon, baking soda, sugar, and salt.
2. In a separate bowl, whisk egg, milk, butter, and vanilla.
3. Pour egg mixture into the flour mixture and mix until well combined.
4. Add strawberries and mix well.
5. Pour batter into the silicone doughnut moulds.
6. Insert a crisper plate in the Ninja Foodi air fryer baskets.
7. Place doughnut moulds in both baskets.
8. Select zone 1, then select "air fry" mode and set the temperature to 320 degrees F for 15 minutes. Press "match" to match zone 2 settings to zone 1. Press "start/stop" to begin.

Nutrition Info:
- (Per serving) Calories 133 | Fat 3.8g | Sodium 339mg | Carbs 21.9g | Fiber 0.8g | Sugar 9.5g | Protein 2.7g

Yellow Potatoes With Eggs

Servings: 2
Cooking Time: 35

Ingredients:
- 1 pound of Dutch yellow potatoes, quartered
- 1 red bell pepper, chopped
- Salt and black pepper, to taste
- 1 green bell pepper, chopped
- 2 teaspoons of olive oil
- 2 teaspoons of garlic powder
- 1 teaspoon of onion powder
- 1 egg
- ¼ teaspoon of butter

Directions:
1. Toss together diced potatoes, green pepper, red pepper, salt, black pepper, and olive oil along with garlic powder and onion powder.
2. Put in the zone 1 basket of the air fryer.
3. Take ramekin and grease it with oil spray.
4. Whisk egg in a bowl and add salt and pepper along with ½ teaspoon of butter.
5. Pour egg into a ramekin and place it in a zone 2 basket.
6. Now start cooking and set a timer for zone 1 basket to 30-35 minutes at 400 degrees at AIR FRY mode.
7. Now for zone 2, set it on AIR FRY mode at 350 degrees F for 8-10 minutes.
8. Press the Smart finish button and press start, it will finish both at the same time.
9. Once done, serve and enjoy.

Nutrition Info:
- (Per serving) Calories 252 | Fat 7.5g | Sodium 37mg | Carbs 40g | Fiber 3.9g | Sugar 7g | Protein 6.7g

Recipe

From the kicthen of

Serves............Prep time............Cook time............

☐ Difficulty   ☐ Easy   ☐ Medium   ☐ Hard

Ingredient

Directions

Snacks And Appetizers Recipes

Bacon Wrapped Tater Tots	18
Beef Jerky Pineapple Jerky	20
Cauliflower Gnocchi	19
Crispy Tortilla Chips	22
Garlic Bread	18
Mexican Jalapeno Poppers	22
Mozzarella Sticks	23
Onion Rings	23
Parmesan Crush Chicken	21
Peppered Asparagus	17
Potato Tater Tots	19
Ravioli	17
Stuffed Bell Peppers	21
Tofu Veggie Meatballs	20

Snacks And Appetizers Recipes

Peppered Asparagus

Servings: 6
Cooking Time: 16 Minutes.

Ingredients:
- 1 bunch of asparagus, trimmed
- Avocado or Olive Oil
- Himalayan salt, to taste
- Black pepper, to taste

Directions:
1. Divide the asparagus in the two crisper plate.
2. Toss the asparagus with salt, black pepper, and oil.
3. Return the crisper plate to the Ninja Foodi Dual Zone Air Fryer.
4. Choose the Air Fry mode for Zone 1 and set the temperature to 390 degrees F and the time to 16 minutes.
5. Select the "MATCH" button to copy the settings for Zone 2.
6. Initiate cooking by pressing the START/STOP button.
7. Serve warm.

Nutrition Info:
- (Per serving) Calories 163 | Fat 11.5g | Sodium 918mg | Carbs 8.3g | Fiber 4.2g | Sugar 0.2g | Protein 7.4g

Ravioli

Servings: 2
Cooking Time: 6 Minutes

Ingredients:
- 12 frozen portions of ravioli
- ½ cup buttermilk
- ½ cup Italian breadcrumbs

Directions:
1. Place two bowls side by side. Put the buttermilk in one and breadcrumbs in the other.
2. Dip each piece of ravioli into the buttermilk then breadcrumbs, making sure to coat them as best as possible.
3. Place a crisper plate in both drawers. In each drawer, put four breaded ravioli pieces in a single layer. Insert the drawers into the unit.
4. Select zone 1, then AIR FRY, then set the temperature to 360 degrees F/ 180 degrees C with a 6-minute timer. To match zone 2 settings to zone 1, choose MATCH. To begin, select START/STOP.
5. Remove the ravioli from the drawers after the timer has finished.

Nutrition Info:
- (Per serving) Calories 481 | Fat 20g | Sodium 1162mg | Carbs 56g | Fiber 4g | Sugar 9g | Protein 19g

Bacon Wrapped Tater Tots

Servings: 8
Cooking Time: 14 Minutes

Ingredients:
- 8 bacon slices
- 3 tablespoons honey
- ½ tablespoon chipotle chile powder
- 16 frozen tater tots

Directions:
1. Cut the bacon slices in half and wrap each tater tot with a bacon slice.
2. Brush the bacon with honey and drizzle chipotle chile powder over them.
3. Insert a toothpick to seal the bacon.
4. Place the wrapped tots in the air fryer baskets.
5. Return the air fryer basket 1 to Zone 1, and basket 2 to Zone 2 of the Ninja Foodi 2-Basket Air Fryer.
6. Choose the "Air Fry" mode for Zone 1 at 350 degrees F and 14 minutes of cooking time.
7. Select the "MATCH COOK" option to copy the settings for Zone 2.
8. Initiate cooking by pressing the START/PAUSE BUTTON.
9. Serve warm.

Nutrition Info:
- (Per serving) Calories 100 | Fat 2g | Sodium 480mg | Carbs 4g | Fiber 2g | Sugar 0g | Protein 18g

Garlic Bread

Servings: 4
Cooking Time: 10 Minutes

Ingredients:
- ½ loaf of bread
- 3 tablespoons butter, softened
- 3 garlic cloves, minced
- ½ teaspoon Italian seasoning
- Small pinch of red pepper flakes
- Optional
- ¼ cup shredded mozzarella cheese
- Freshly grated parmesan cheese
- Chopped fresh parsley for serving/topping

Directions:
1. Slice the bread in half horizontally or as appropriate to fit inside the air fryer.
2. Combine the softened butter, garlic, Italian seasoning, and red pepper flakes in a mixing bowl.
3. Brush the garlic butter mixture evenly over the bread.
4. Place a crisper plate in each drawer. Place the bread pieces into each drawer. Insert the drawers into the unit.
5. Select zone 1, then AIR FRY, then set the temperature to 360 degrees F/ 180 degrees C with a 6-minute timer. To match zone 2 settings to zone 1, choose MATCH. To begin, select START/STOP.
6. Remove the garlic bread from your air fryer, slice, and serve!

Nutrition Info:
- (Per serving) Calories 150 | Fat 8.2g | Sodium 208mg | Carbs 14.3g | Fiber 2.3g | Sugar 1.2g | Protein 4.9g

Potato Tater Tots

Servings: 4
Cooking Time: 27 Minutes.

Ingredients:
- 2 potatoes, peeled
- ½ teaspoon Cajun seasoning
- Olive oil cooking spray
- Sea salt to taste

Directions:
1. Boil water in a cooking pot and cook potatoes in it for 15 minutes.
2. Drain and leave the potatoes to cool in a bowl.
3. Grate these potatoes and toss them with Cajun seasoning.
4. Make small tater tots out of this mixture.
5. Divide them into the two crisper plates and spray them with cooking oil.
6. Return the crisper plates to the Ninja Foodi Dual Zone Air Fryer.
7. Choose the Air Fry mode for Zone 1 and set the temperature to 375 degrees F and the time to 27 minutes.
8. Select the "MATCH" button to copy the settings for Zone 2.
9. Initiate cooking by pressing the START/STOP button.
10. Flip them once cooked halfway through, and resume cooking.
11. Serve warm

Nutrition Info:
- (Per serving) Calories 185 | Fat 11g | Sodium 355mg | Carbs 21g | Fiber 5.8g | Sugar 3g | Protein 4.7g

Cauliflower Gnocchi

Servings: 5
Cooking Time: 17 Minutes.

Ingredients:
- 1 bag frozen cauliflower gnocchi
- 1 ½ tablespoons olive oil
- 1 teaspoon garlic powder
- 3 tablespoons parmesan, grated
- ½ teaspoon dried basil
- Salt to taste
- Fresh chopped parsley for topping

Directions:
1. Toss gnocchi with olive oil, garlic powder, 1 tablespoon of parmesan, salt, and basil in a bowl.
2. Divide the gnocchi in the two crisper plate.
3. Return the crisper plate to the Ninja Foodi Dual Zone Air Fryer.
4. Choose the Air Fry mode for Zone 1 and set the temperature to 400 degrees F and the time to 10 minutes.
5. Select the "MATCH" button to copy the settings for Zone 2.
6. Initiate cooking by pressing the START/STOP button.
7. Toss the gnocchi once cooked halfway through, then resume cooking.
8. Drizzle the remaining parmesan on top of the gnocchi and cook again for 7 minutes.
9. Serve warm.

Nutrition Info:
- (Per serving) Calories 134 | Fat 5.9g | Sodium 343mg | Carbs 9.5g | Fiber 0.5g | Sugar 1.1g | Protein 10.4g

Beef Jerky Pineapple Jerky

Servings: 8
Cooking Time: 6 To 12 Hours

Ingredients:
- FOR THE BEEF JERKY
- ½ cup reduced-sodium soy sauce
- ¼ cup pineapple juice
- 1 tablespoon dark brown sugar
- 1 tablespoon Worcestershire sauce
- ½ teaspoon smoked paprika
- ¼ teaspoon freshly ground black pepper
- ¼ teaspoon red pepper flakes
- 1 pound beef bottom round, trimmed of excess fat, cut into ¼-inch-thick slices
- FOR THE PINEAPPLE JERKY
- 1 pound pineapple, cut into ⅛-inch-thick rounds, pat dry
- 1 teaspoon chili powder (optional)

Directions:
1. To prep the beef jerky: In a large zip-top bag, combine the soy sauce, pineapple juice, brown sugar, Worcestershire sauce, smoked paprika, black pepper, and red pepper flakes.
2. Add the beef slices, seal the bag, and toss to coat the meat in the marinade. Refrigerate overnight or for at least 8 hours.
3. Remove the beef slices and discard the marinade. Using a paper towel, pat the slices dry to remove excess marinade.
4. To prep the pineapple jerky: Sprinkle the pineapple with chili powder (if using).
5. To dehydrate the jerky: Arrange half of the beef slices in a single layer in the Zone 1 basket, making sure they do not overlap. Place a crisper plate on top of the beef slices and arrange the remaining slices in a single layer on top of the crisper plate. Insert the basket in the unit.
6. Repeat this process with the pineapple in the Zone 2 basket and insert the basket in the unit.
7. Select Zone 1, select DEHYDRATE, set the temperature to 150°F, and set the time to 8 hours.
8. Select Zone 2, select DEHYDRATE, set the temperature to 135°F, and set the time to 12 hours.
9. Press START/PAUSE to begin cooking.
10. When the Zone 1 timer reads 2 hours, press START/PAUSE. Remove the basket and check the beef jerky for doneness. If necessary, reinsert the basket and press START/PAUSE to resume cooking.

Nutrition Info:
- (Per serving) Calories: 171; Total fat: 6.5g; Saturated fat: 2g; Carbohydrates: 2g; Fiber: 0g; Protein: 25g; Sodium: 369mg

Tofu Veggie Meatballs

Servings: 4
Cooking Time: 10minutes

Ingredients:
- 122g firm tofu, drained
- 50g breadcrumbs
- 37g bamboo shoots, thinly sliced
- 22g carrots, shredded & steamed
- 1 tsp garlic powder
- 1 ½ tbsp soy sauce
- 2 tbsp cornstarch
- 3 dried shitake mushrooms, soaked & chopped
- Pepper
- Salt

Directions:
1. Add tofu and remaining ingredients into the food processor and process until well combined.
2. Insert a crisper plate in the Ninja Foodi air fryer baskets.
3. Make small balls from the tofu mixture and place them in both baskets.
4. Select zone 1, then select "air fry" mode and set the temperature to 380 degrees F for 10 minutes. Press "match" to match zone 2 settings to zone 1. Press "start/stop" to begin. Turn halfway through.

Nutrition Info:
- (Per serving) Calories 125 | Fat 1.8g |Sodium 614mg | Carbs 23.4g | Fiber 2.5g | Sugar 3.8g | Protein 5.3g

Stuffed Bell Peppers

Servings: 3
Cooking Time: 16

Ingredients:
- 6 large bell peppers
- 1-1/2 cup cooked rice
- 2 cups cheddar cheese

Directions:
1. Cut the bell peppers in half lengthwise and remove all the seeds.
2. Fill the cavity of each bell pepper with cooked rice.
3. Divide the bell peppers amongst the two zones of the air fryer basket.
4. Set the time for zone 1 for 200 degrees for 10 minutes.
5. Select MATCH button of zone 2 basket.
6. Afterward, take out the baskets and sprinkle cheese on top.
7. Set the time for zone 1 for 200 degrees for 6 minutes.
8. Select MATCH button of zone 2 basket.
9. Once it's done, serve.

Nutrition Info:
- (Per serving) Calories 605| Fat 26g | Sodium477 mg | Carbs68.3 g | Fiber4 g| Sugar 12.5g | Protein25.6 g

Parmesan Crush Chicken

Servings: 4
Cooking Time: 18

Ingredients:
- 4 chicken breasts
- 1 cup parmesan cheese
- 1 cup bread crumb
- 2 eggs, whisked
- Salt, to taste
- Oil spray, for greasing

Directions:
1. Whisk egg in a large bowl and set aside.
2. Season the chicken breast with salt and then put it in egg wash.
3. Next, dredge it in breadcrumb then parmesan cheese.
4. Line both the basket of the air fryer with parchment paper.
5. Divided the breast pieces between the backsets, and oil spray the breast pieces.
6. Set zone 1 basket to air fry mode at 350 degrees F for 18 minutes.
7. Select the MATCH button for the zone 2 basket.
8. Once it's done, serve.

Nutrition Info:
- (Per serving) Calories574 | Fat25g | Sodium848 mg | Carbs 21.4g | Fiber 1.2g| Sugar 1.8g | Protein 64.4g

Mexican Jalapeno Poppers

Servings: 8
Cooking Time: 5minutes

Ingredients:
- 5 jalapenos, cut in half & remove seeds
- ¼ tsp red pepper flakes, crushed
- 1 tsp onion powder
- 32g salsa
- 113g goat cheese
- 1 tsp garlic powder
- Pepper
- Salt

Directions:
1. In a small bowl, mix goat cheese, salsa, red pepper flakes, onion powder, garlic powder, pepper, and salt.
2. Stuff each jalapeno half with goat cheese mixture.
3. Insert a crisper plate in the Ninja Foodi air fryer baskets.
4. Place stuffed peppers in both baskets.
5. Select zone 1 then select "air fry" mode and set the temperature to 360 degrees F for 8 minutes—Press "match" to match zone 2 settings to zone 1. Press "start/stop" to begin.

Nutrition Info:
- (Per serving) Calories 112 | Fat 8.2g |Sodium 148mg | Carbs 2.6g | Fiber 0.6g | Sugar 1.5g | Protein 7.4g

Crispy Tortilla Chips

Servings: 8
Cooking Time: 13 Minutes.

Ingredients:
- 4 (6-inch) corn tortillas
- 1 tablespoon Avocado Oil
- Sea salt to taste
- Cooking spray

Directions:
1. Spread the corn tortillas on the working surface.
2. Slice them into bite-sized triangles.
3. Toss them with salt and cooking oil.
4. Divide the triangles in the two crisper plates into a single layer.
5. Return the crisper plates to the Ninja Foodi Dual Zone Air Fryer.
6. Choose the Air Fry mode for Zone 1 and set the temperature to 390 degrees F and the time to 13 minutes.
7. Select the "MATCH" button to copy the settings for Zone 2.
8. Initiate cooking by pressing the START/STOP button.
9. Toss the chips once cooked halfway through, then resume cooking.
10. Serve and enjoy.

Nutrition Info:
- (Per serving) Calories 103 | Fat 8.4g |Sodium 117mg | Carbs 3.5g | Fiber 0.9g | Sugar 1.5g | Protein 5.1g

Onion Rings

Servings: 4
Cooking Time: 7 Minutes

Ingredients:
- 170g onion, sliced into rings
- ½ cup breadcrumbs
- 2 eggs, beaten
- ½ cup flour
- Salt and black pepper to taste

Directions:
1. Mix flour, black pepper and salt in a bowl.
2. Dredge the onion rings through the flour mixture.
3. Dip them in the eggs and coat with the breadcrumbs.
4. Place the coated onion rings in the air fryer baskets.
5. Return the air fryer basket 1 to Zone 1, and basket 2 to Zone 2 of the Ninja Foodi 2-Basket Air Fryer.
6. Choose the "Air Fry" mode for Zone 1 at 350 degrees F and 7 minutes of cooking time.
7. Select the "MATCH COOK" option to copy the settings for Zone 2.
8. Initiate cooking by pressing the START/PAUSE BUTTON.
9. Shake the rings once cooked halfway through.
10. Serve warm.

Nutrition Info:
- (Per serving) Calories 185 | Fat 11g | Sodium 355mg | Carbs 21g | Fiber 5.8g | Sugar 3g | Protein 4.7g

Mozzarella Sticks

Servings: 8
Cooking Time: 1 Hour 15 Minutes

Ingredients:
- 8 mozzarella sticks
- ¼ cup all-purpose flour
- 1 egg, whisked
- 1 cup panko breadcrumbs
- ½ teaspoon each onion powder, garlic powder, smoked paprika, salt

Directions:
1. Freeze the mozzarella sticks for 30 minutes after placing them on a parchment-lined plate.
2. In the meantime, set up your "breading station": Fill a Ziploc bag halfway with flour. In a small dish, whisk the egg. In a separate shallow bowl, combine the panko and spices.
3. To bread your mozzarella sticks: Toss the sticks into the bag of flour, seal it, and shake to coat the cheese evenly. Take out the sticks and dip them in the egg, then in the panko, one at a time. Put the coated sticks back on the plate and put them in the freezer for another 30 minutes.
4. Place a crisper plate in each drawer, then add the mozzarella sticks in a single layer to each. Insert the drawers into the unit.
5. Select zone 1, then AIR FRY, then set the temperature to 400 degrees F/ 200 degrees C with a 15-minute timer. To match zone 2 settings to zone 1, choose MATCH. To begin, select START/STOP

Nutrition Info:
- (Per serving) Calories 131 | Fat 5.3g | Sodium 243mg | Carbs 11.3g | Fiber 1.1g | Sugar 0.3g | Protein 9.9g

Vegetables And Sides Recipes

Acorn Squash Slices	27
Air Fried Okra	29
Air Fryer Vegetables	31
Beets With Orange Gremolata And Goat's Cheese	30
Garlic Herbed Baked Potatoes	25
Garlic Potato Wedges In Air Fryer	29
Garlic-herb Fried Squash	30
Garlic-rosemary Brussels Sprouts	26
Herb And Lemon Cauliflower	25
Jerk Tofu With Roasted Cabbage	27
Pepper Poppers	26
Potatoes & Beans	28
Spanakopita Rolls With Mediterranean Vegetable Salad	28
Zucchini With Stuffing	31

Vegetables And Sides Recipes

Herb And Lemon Cauliflower

Servings: 4
Cooking Time: 10 Minutes

Ingredients:
- 1 cauliflower head, cut into florets
- 4 tablespoons olive oil
- ¼ cup fresh parsley
- 1 tablespoon fresh rosemary
- 1 tablespoon fresh thyme
- 1 teaspoon lemon zest, grated
- 2 tablespoons lemon juice
- ½ teaspoon salt
- ¼ teaspoon crushed red pepper flakes

Directions:
1. Toss cauliflower with oil, herbs and the rest of the ingredients in a bowl.
2. Divide the seasoned cauliflower in the air fryer baskets.
3. Return the air fryer basket 1 to Zone 1, and basket 2 to Zone 2 of the Ninja Foodi 2-Basket Air Fryer.
4. Choose the "Air Fry" mode for Zone 1 at 350 degrees F and 10 minutes of cooking time.
5. Select the "MATCH COOK" option to copy the settings for Zone 2.
6. Initiate cooking by pressing the START/PAUSE BUTTON.
7. Serve warm.

Nutrition Info:
- (Per serving) Calories 212 | Fat 11.8g | Sodium 321mg | Carbs 24.6g | Fiber 4.4g | Sugar 8g | Protein 7.3g

Garlic Herbed Baked Potatoes

Servings: 4
Cooking Time: 45

Ingredients:
- 4 large baking potatoes
- Salt and black pepper, to taste
- 2 teaspoons of avocado oil
- Cheese ingredients
- 2 cups sour cream
- 1 teaspoon of garlic clove, minced
- 1 teaspoon fresh dill
- 2 teaspoons chopped chives
- Salt and black pepper, to taste
- 2 teaspoons Worcestershire sauce

Directions:
1. Pierce the skin of potatoes with a fork.
2. Season the potatoes with olive oil, salt, and black pepper.
3. Divide the potatoes among two baskets of the ninja air fryer.
4. Now hit 1 for the first basket and set it to AIR FRY mode at 350 degrees F, for 45 minutes.
5. Select the MATCH button for zone 2.
6. Meanwhile, take a bowl and mix all the ingredient under cheese ingredients
7. Once the cooking cycle complete, take out and make a slit in-between the potatoes.
8. Add cheese mixture in the cavity and serve it hot.

Nutrition Info:
- (Per serving) Calories 382 | Fat 24.6 g | Sodium 107mg | Carbs 36.2g | Fiber 2.5g | Sugar 2 g | Protein 7.3g

Garlic-rosemary Brussels Sprouts

Servings: 4
Cooking Time: 8 Minutes

Ingredients:
- 3 tablespoons olive oil
- 2 garlic cloves, minced
- ½ teaspoon salt
- ¼ teaspoon black pepper
- 455g Brussels sprouts, halved
- ½ cup panko bread crumbs
- 1-½ teaspoons rosemary, minced

Directions:
1. Toss the Brussels sprouts with crumbs and the rest of the ingredients in a bowl.
2. Divide the sprouts into the Ninja Foodi 2 Baskets Air Fryer baskets.
3. Return the air fryer basket 1 to Zone 1, and basket 2 to Zone 2 of the Ninja Foodi 2-Basket Air Fryer.
4. Choose the "Air Fry" mode for Zone 1 at 350 degrees F and 8 minutes of cooking time.
5. Select the "MATCH COOK" option to copy the settings for Zone 2.
6. Initiate cooking by pressing the START/PAUSE BUTTON.
7. Toss the Brussels sprouts once cooked halfway through.
8. Serve warm.

Nutrition Info:
- (Per serving) Calories 231 | Fat 9g |Sodium 271mg | Carbs 32.8g | Fiber 6.4g | Sugar 7g | Protein 6.3g

Pepper Poppers

Servings: 24
Cooking Time: 20 Minutes

Ingredients:
- 8 ounces cream cheese, softened
- ¾ cup shredded cheddar cheese
- ¾ cup shredded Monterey Jack cheese
- 6 bacon strips, cooked and crumbled
- ¼ teaspoon salt
- ¼ teaspoon garlic powder
- ¼ teaspoon chili powder
- ¼ teaspoon smoked paprika
- 1-pound fresh jalapeño peppers, halved lengthwise and deseeded
- ½ cup dry breadcrumbs
- Sour cream, French onion dip, or ranch salad dressing (optional)

Directions:
1. In a large bowl, combine the cheeses, bacon, and seasonings; mix well. Spoon 1½ to 2 tablespoons of the mixture into each pepper half. Roll them in the breadcrumbs.
2. Place a crisper plate in each drawer. Put the prepared peppers in a single layer in each drawer. Insert the drawers into the unit.
3. Select zone 1, then AIR FRY, then set the temperature to 360 degrees F/ 180 degrees C with a 20-minute timer. To match zone 2 settings to zone 1, choose MATCH. To begin, select START/STOP.
4. Remove the peppers from the drawers after the timer has finished.

Nutrition Info:
- (Per serving) Calories 81 | Fat 6g | Sodium 145mg | Carbs 3g | Fiber 4g | Sugar 1g | Protein 3g

Jerk Tofu With Roasted Cabbage

Servings: 4
Cooking Time: 20 Minutes

Ingredients:
- FOR THE JERK TOFU
- 1 (14-ounce) package extra-firm tofu, drained
- 1 tablespoon apple cider vinegar
- 1 tablespoon reduced-sodium soy sauce
- 2 tablespoons jerk seasoning
- Juice of 1 lime
- ½ teaspoon kosher salt
- 2 tablespoons olive oil
- FOR THE CABBAGE
- 1 (14-ounce) bag coleslaw mix
- 1 red bell pepper, thinly sliced
- 2 scallions, thinly sliced
- 2 tablespoons water
- 3 garlic cloves, minced
- ¼ teaspoon fresh thyme leaves
- ¼ teaspoon onion powder
- ¼ teaspoon kosher salt
- ¼ teaspoon freshly ground black pepper

Directions:
1. To prep the jerk tofu: Cut the tofu horizontally into 4 slabs.
2. In a shallow dish (big enough to hold the tofu slabs), whisk together the vinegar, soy sauce, jerk seasoning, lime juice, and salt.
3. Place the tofu in the marinade and turn to coat both sides. Cover and marinate for at least 15 minutes (or up to overnight in the refrigerator).
4. To prep the cabbage: In the Zone 2 basket, combine the coleslaw, bell pepper, scallions, water, garlic, thyme, onion powder, salt, and black pepper.
5. To cook the tofu and cabbage: Install a crisper plate in the Zone 1 basket and add the tofu in a single layer. Brush the tofu with the oil and insert the basket in the unit. Insert the Zone 2 basket in the unit.
6. Select Zone 1, select AIR FRY, set the temperature to 390°F, and set the timer to 15 minutes.
7. Select Zone 2, select ROAST, set the temperature to 330°F, and set the timer to 20 minutes. Select SMART FINISH.
8. Press START/PAUSE to begin cooking.
9. When both timers read 5 minutes, press START/PAUSE. Remove the Zone 1 basket and use silicone-tipped tongs to flip the tofu. Reinsert the basket in the unit. Remove the Zone 2 basket and stir the cabbage. Reinsert the basket and press START/PAUSE to resume cooking.
10. When cooking is complete, the tofu will be crispy and browned around the edges and the cabbage soft.
11. Transfer the tofu to four plates and serve with the cabbage on the side.

Nutrition Info:
- (Per serving) Calories: 220; Total fat: 12g; Saturated fat: 1.5g; Carbohydrates: 21g; Fiber: 5g; Protein: 12g; Sodium: 817mg

Acorn Squash Slices

Servings: 6
Cooking Time: 10 Minutes

Ingredients:
- 2 medium acorn squashes
- ⅔ cup packed brown sugar
- ½ cup butter, melted

Directions:
1. Cut the squash in half, remove the seeds and slice into ½ inch slices.
2. Place the squash slices in the air fryer baskets.
3. Drizzle brown sugar and butter over the squash slices.
4. Return the air fryer basket 1 to Zone 1, and basket 2 to Zone 2 of the Ninja Foodi 2-Basket Air Fryer.
5. Choose the "Air Fry" mode for Zone 1 and set the temperature to 350 degrees F and 10 minutes of cooking time.
6. Select the "MATCH COOK" option to copy the settings for Zone 2.
7. Initiate cooking by pressing the START/PAUSE BUTTON.
8. Flip the squash once cooked halfway through.
9. Serve.

Nutrition Info:
- (Per serving) Calories 206 | Fat 3.4g | Sodium 174mg | Carbs 35g | Fiber 9.4g | Sugar 5.9g | Protein 10.6g

Spanakopita Rolls With Mediterranean Vegetable Salad

Servings: 4
Cooking Time: 15 Minutes

Ingredients:
- FOR THE SPANAKOPITA ROLLS
- 1 (10-ounce) package chopped frozen spinach, thawed
- 4 ounces feta cheese, crumbled
- 2 large eggs
- 1 teaspoon dried oregano
- ½ teaspoon freshly ground black pepper
- 12 sheets phyllo dough, thawed
- Nonstick cooking spray
- FOR THE ROASTED VEGETABLES
- 1 medium eggplant, diced
- 1 small red onion, cut into 8 wedges
- 1 red bell pepper, sliced
- 2 tablespoons olive oil
- FOR THE SALAD
- 1 (15-ounce) can chickpeas, drained and rinsed
- ¼ cup chopped fresh parsley
- ¼ cup olive oil
- ¼ cup red wine vinegar
- 2 garlic cloves, minced
- ½ teaspoon dried oregano
- ¼ teaspoon kosher salt
- ¼ teaspoon freshly ground black pepper

Directions:
1. To prep the spanakopita rolls: Squeeze as much liquid from the spinach as you can and place the spinach in a large bowl. Add the feta, eggs, oregano, and black pepper. Mix well.
2. Lay one sheet of phyllo on a clean work surface and mist it with cooking spray. Place another sheet of phyllo directly on top of the first sheet and mist it with cooking spray. Repeat with a third sheet.
3. Spoon one-quarter of the spinach mixture along one short side of the phyllo. Fold the long sides in over the spinach, then roll up it like a burrito.
4. Repeat this process with the remaining phyllo sheets and spinach mixture to form 4 rolls.
5. To prep the vegetables: In a large bowl, combine the eggplant, onion, bell pepper, and oil. Mix well.
6. To cook the rolls and vegetables: Install a crisper plate in each of the two baskets. Place the spanakopita rolls seam-side down in the Zone 1 basket, and spritz the rolls with cooking spray. Place the vegetables in the Zone 2 basket and insert both baskets in the unit.
7. Select Zone 1, select AIR FRY, set the temperature to 375°F, and set the timer to 10 minutes.
8. Select Zone 2, select ROAST, set the temperature to 375°F, and set the timer to 15 minutes. Select SMART FINISH.
9. Press START/PAUSE to begin cooking.
10. When the Zone 1 timer reads 3 minutes, press START/PAUSE. Remove the basket and use silicone-tipped tongs or a spatula to flip the spanakopita rolls. Reinsert the basket and press START/PAUSE to resume cooking.
11. When cooking is complete, the rolls should be crisp and golden brown and the vegetables tender.
12. To assemble the salad: Transfer the roasted vegetables to a large bowl. Stir in the chickpeas and parsley.
13. In a small bowl, whisk together the oil, vinegar, garlic, oregano, salt, and black pepper. Pour the dressing over the vegetables and toss to coat. Serve warm.

Nutrition Info:
- (Per serving) Calories: 739; Total fat: 51g; Saturated fat: 8g; Carbohydrates: 67g; Fiber: 11g; Protein: 21g; Sodium: 806mg

Potatoes & Beans

Servings: 4
Cooking Time: 25 Minutes

Ingredients:
- 453g potatoes, cut into pieces
- 15ml olive oil
- 1 tsp garlic powder
- 160g green beans, trimmed
- Pepper
- Salt

Directions:
1. In a bowl, toss green beans, garlic powder, potatoes, oil, pepper, and salt.
2. Insert a crisper plate in the Ninja Foodi air fryer baskets.
3. Add green beans and potato mixture to both baskets.
4. Select zone 1 then select "air fry" mode and set the temperature to 380 degrees F for 25 minutes. Press "match" to match zone 2 settings to zone 1. Press "start/stop" to begin. Stir halfway through.

Nutrition Info:
- (Per serving) Calories 128 | Fat 3.7g |Sodium 49mg | Carbs 22.4g | Fiber 4.7g | Sugar 2.3g | Protein 3.1g

Air Fried Okra

Servings: 2
Cooking Time: 13 Minutes.

Ingredients:
- ½ lb. okra pods sliced
- 1 teaspoon olive oil
- ¼ teaspoon salt
- ⅛ teaspoon black pepper

Directions:
1. Preheat the Ninja Foodi Dual Zone Air Fryer to 350 degrees F.
2. Toss okra with olive oil, salt, and black pepper in a bowl.
3. Spread the okra in a single layer in the two crisper plates.
4. Return the crisper plate to the Ninja Foodi Dual Zone Air Fryer.
5. Choose the Air Fry mode for Zone 1 and set the temperature to 375 degrees F and the time to 13 minutes.
6. Select the "MATCH" button to copy the settings for Zone 2.
7. Initiate cooking by pressing the START/STOP button.
8. Toss the okra once cooked halfway through, and resume cooking.
9. Serve warm.

Nutrition Info:
- (Per serving) Calories 208 | Fat 5g | Sodium 1205mg | Carbs 34.1g | Fiber 7.8g | Sugar 2.5g | Protein 5.9g

Garlic Potato Wedges In Air Fryer

Servings: 2
Cooking Time: 23

Ingredients:
- 4 medium potatoes, peeled and cut into wedges
- 4 tablespoons of butter
- 1 teaspoon of chopped cilantro
- 1 cup plain flour
- 1 teaspoon of garlic, minced
- Salt and black pepper, to taste

Directions:
1. Soak the potatoes wedges in cold water for about 30 minutes.
2. Then drain and pat dry with a paper towel.
3. Boil water in a large pot and boil the wedges just for 3 minutes.
4. Then take it out on a paper towel.
5. Now in a bowl mix garlic, melted butter, salt, pepper, cilantro and whisk it well.
6. Add the flour to a separate bowl and add salt and black pepper.
7. Then add water to the flour so it gets runny in texture.
8. Now, coat the potatoes with flour mixture and add it to two foil tins.
9. Put foil tins in both the air fryer basket.
10. Now, set time for zone 1 basket using AIRFRY mode at 390 degrees F for 20 minutes.
11. Select the MATCH button for the zone 2 basket.
12. Once done, serve and enjoy.

Nutrition Info:
- (Per serving) Calories 727 | Fat 24.1g | Sodium 191mg | Carbs 115.1g | Fiber 12g | Sugar 5.1g | Protein 14 g

Garlic-herb Fried Squash

Servings: 4
Cooking Time: 15 Minutes

Ingredients:
- 5 cups halved small pattypan squash (about 1¼ pounds)
- 1 tablespoon olive oil
- 2 garlic cloves, minced
- ½ teaspoon salt
- ¼ teaspoon dried oregano
- ¼ teaspoon dried thyme
- ¼ teaspoon pepper
- 1 tablespoon minced fresh parsley, for serving

Directions:
1. Place the squash in a large bowl.
2. Mix the oil, garlic, salt, oregano, thyme, and pepper; drizzle over the squash. Toss to coat.
3. Place a crisper plate in both drawers. Put the squash in a single layer in each drawer. Insert the drawers into the unit.
4. Select zone 1, then AIR FRY, then set the temperature to 360 degrees F/ 180 degrees C with a 6-minute timer. To match zone 2 settings to zone 1, choose MATCH. To begin, select START/STOP.
5. Remove the squash from the drawers after the timer has finished. Sprinkle with the parsley.

Nutrition Info:
- (Per serving) Calories 58 | Fat 3g | Sodium 296mg | Carbs 6g | Fiber 2g | Sugar 3g | Protein 2g

Beets With Orange Gremolata And Goat's Cheese

Servings: 12
Cooking Time: 45 Minutes

Ingredients:
- 3 medium fresh golden beets (about 1 pound)
- 3 medium fresh beets (about 1 pound)
- 2 tablespoons lime juice
- 2 tablespoons orange juice
- ½ teaspoon fine sea salt
- 1 tablespoon minced fresh parsley
- 1 tablespoon minced fresh sage
- 1 garlic clove, minced
- 1 teaspoon grated orange zest
- 3 tablespoons crumbled goat's cheese
- 2 tablespoons sunflower kernels

Directions:
1. Scrub the beets and trim the tops by 1 inch.
2. Place the beets on a double thickness of heavy-duty foil (about 24 x 12 inches). Fold the foil around the beets, sealing tightly.
3. Place a crisper plate in both drawers. Put the beets in a single layer in each drawer. Insert the drawers into the unit.
4. Select zone 1, then AIR FRY, then set the temperature to 360 degrees F/ 180 degrees C with a 45-minute timer. To match zone 2 settings to zone 1, choose MATCH. To begin, select START/STOP.
5. Remove the beets from the drawers after the timer has finished. Peel, halve, and slice them when they're cool enough to handle. Place them in a serving bowl.
6. Toss in the lime juice, orange juice, and salt to coat. Sprinkle the beets with the parsley, sage, garlic, and orange zest. The sunflower kernels and goat's cheese go on top.

Nutrition Info:
- (Per serving) Calories 481 | Fat 20g | Sodium 1162mg | Carbs 56g | Fiber 4g | Sugar 9g | Protein 19g

Air Fryer Vegetables

Servings: 2
Cooking Time: 15 Minutes

Ingredients:
- 1 courgette, diced
- 2 capsicums, diced
- 1 head broccoli, diced
- 1 red onion, diced
- Marinade
- 1 teaspoon smoked paprika
- 1 teaspoon garlic granules
- 1 teaspoon Herb de Provence
- Salt and black pepper, to taste
- 1½ tablespoon olive oil
- 2 tablespoons lemon juice

Directions:
1. Toss the veggies with the rest of the marinade ingredients in a bowl.
2. Spread the veggies in the air fryer baskets.
3. Return the air fryer basket 1 to Zone 1, and basket 2 to Zone 2 of the Ninja Foodi 2-Basket Air Fryer.
4. Choose the "Air Fry" mode for Zone 1 at 400 degrees F and 15 minutes of cooking time.
5. Select the "MATCH COOK" option to copy the settings for Zone 2.
6. Initiate cooking by pressing the START/PAUSE BUTTON.
7. Toss the veggies once cooked half way through.
8. Serve warm.

Nutrition Info:
- (Per serving) Calories 166 | Fat 3.2g | Sodium 437mg | Carbs 28.8g | Fiber 1.8g | Sugar 2.7g | Protein 5.8g

Zucchini With Stuffing

Servings: 3
Cooking Time: 20

Ingredients:
- 1 cup quinoa, rinsed
- 1 cup black olives
- 6 medium zucchinis, about 2 pounds
- 2 cups cannellini beans, drained
- 1 white onion, chopped
- ¼ cup almonds, chopped
- 4 cloves of garlic, chopped
- 4 tablespoons olive oil
- 1 cup of water
- 2 cups Parmesan cheese, for topping

Directions:
1. First wash the zucchini and cut it lengthwise.
2. Take a skillet and heat oil in it
3. Sauté the onion in olive oil for a few minutes.
4. Then add the quinoa and water and let it cook for 8 minutes with the lid on the top.
5. Transfer the quinoa to a bowl and add all remaining ingredients excluding zucchini and Parmesan cheese.
6. Scoop out the seeds of zucchinis.
7. Fill the cavity of zucchinis with bowl mixture.
8. Top it with a handful of Parmesan cheese.
9. Arrange 4 zucchinis in both air fryer baskets.
10. Select zone1 basket at AIR FRY for 20 minutes and adjusting the temperature to 390 degrees F.
11. Use the Match button to select the same setting for zone 2.
12. Serve and enjoy.

Nutrition Info:
- (Per serving) Calories 1171 | Fat 48.6g | Sodium 1747mg | Carbs 132.4g | Fiber 42.1g | Sugar 11.5g | Protein 65.7g

Beef, Pork, And Lamb Recipes

Air Fried Lamb Chops 37

Asian Pork Skewers 33

Beef & Broccoli 38

Cinnamon-apple Pork Chops 34

Italian-style Meatballs With Garlicky Roasted Broccoli 36

Juicy Pork Chops 39

Korean Bbq Beef 39

Lamb Chops With Dijon Garlic 37

Lamb Shank With Mushroom Sauce 34

Meatloaf 36

Mustard Rubbed Lamb Chops 35

Parmesan Pork Chops 33

Pork Tenderloin With Brown Sugar–pecan Sweet Potatoes 35

Steak And Mashed Creamy Potatoes 38

Beef, Pork, And Lamb Recipes

Asian Pork Skewers

Servings: 4
Cooking Time: 25 Minutes

Ingredients:
- 450g pork shoulder, sliced
- 30g ginger, peeled and crushed
- ½ tablespoon crushed garlic
- 67½ml soy sauce
- 22½ml honey
- 22½ml rice vinegar
- 10ml toasted sesame oil
- 8 skewers

Directions:
1. Pound the pork slices with a mallet.
2. Mix ginger, garlic, soy sauce, honey, rice vinegar, and sesame oil in a bowl.
3. Add pork slices to the marinade and mix well to coat.
4. Cover and marinate the pork for 30 minutes.
5. Thread the pork on the wooden skewers and place them in the air fryer baskets.
6. Return the air fryer basket 1 to Zone 1, and basket 2 to Zone 2 of the Ninja Foodi 2-Basket Air Fryer.
7. Choose the "Air Fry" mode for Zone 1 and set the temperature to 350 degrees F and 25 minutes of cooking time.
8. Select the "MATCH COOK" option to copy the settings for Zone 2.
9. Initiate cooking by pressing the START/PAUSE BUTTON.
10. Flip the skewers once cooked halfway through.
11. Serve warm.

Nutrition Info:
- (Per serving) Calories 400 | Fat 32g |Sodium 721mg | Carbs 2.6g | Fiber 0g | Sugar 0g | Protein 27.4g

Parmesan Pork Chops

Servings: 4
Cooking Time: 15 Minutes.

Ingredients:
- 4 boneless pork chops
- 2 tablespoons olive oil
- ½ cup freshly grated Parmesan
- 1 teaspoon salt
- 1 teaspoon paprika
- 1 teaspoon garlic powder
- 1 teaspoon onion powder
- ½ teaspoon black pepper

Directions:
1. Pat dry the pork chops with a paper towel and rub them with olive oil.
2. Mix parmesan with spices in a medium bowl.
3. Rub the pork chops with Parmesan mixture.
4. Place 2 seasoned pork chops in each of the two crisper plate
5. Return the crisper plate to the Ninja Foodi Dual Zone Air Fryer.
6. Choose the Air Fry mode for Zone 1 and set the temperature to 390 degrees F and the time to 15 minutes.
7. Select the "MATCH" button to copy the settings for Zone 2.
8. Initiate cooking by pressing the START/STOP button.
9. Flip the pork chops when cooked halfway through, then resume cooking.
10. Serve warm.

Nutrition Info:
- (Per serving) Calories 396 | Fat 23.2g |Sodium 622mg | Carbs 0.7g | Fiber 0g | Sugar 0g | Protein 45.6g

Cinnamon-apple Pork Chops

Servings: 4
Cooking Time: 10 Minutes

Ingredients:
- 2 tablespoons butter
- 4 boneless pork loin chops
- 3 tablespoons brown sugar
- 1 teaspoon ground cinnamon
- ½ teaspoon ground nutmeg
- ¼ teaspoon salt
- 4 medium tart apples, sliced
- 2 tablespoons chopped pecans

Directions:
1. Mix butter, brown sugar, cinnamon, nutmeg, and salt in a bowl.
2. Rub this mixture over the pork chops and place them in the air fryer baskets.
3. Top them with apples and pecans.
4. Return the air fryer basket 1 to Zone 1, and basket 2 to Zone 2 of the Ninja Foodi 2-Basket Air Fryer.
5. Choose the "Air Fry" mode for Zone 1 at 375 degrees F and 10 minutes of cooking time.
6. Select the "MATCH COOK" option to copy the settings for Zone 2.
7. Initiate cooking by pressing the START/PAUSE BUTTON.
8. Serve warm.

Nutrition Info:
- (Per serving) Calories 316 | Fat 17g | Sodium 271mg | Carbs 4.3g | Fiber 0.9g | Sugar 2.1g | Protein 35g

Lamb Shank With Mushroom Sauce

Servings: 4
Cooking Time: 35 Minutes.

Ingredients:
- 20 mushrooms, chopped
- 2 red bell pepper, chopped
- 2 red onion, chopped
- 1 cup red wine
- 4 leeks, chopped
- 6 tablespoons balsamic vinegar
- 2 teaspoons black pepper
- 2 teaspoons salt
- 3 tablespoons fresh rosemary
- 6 garlic cloves
- 4 lamb shanks
- 3 tablespoons olive oil

Directions:
1. Season the lamb shanks with salt, pepper, rosemary, and 1 teaspoon of olive oil.
2. Set half of the shanks in each of the crisper plate.
3. Return the crisper plate to the Ninja Foodi Dual Zone Air Fryer.
4. Choose the Air Fry mode for Zone 1 and set the temperature to 390 degrees F and the time to 25 minutes.
5. Select the "MATCH" button to copy the settings for Zone 2.
6. Initiate cooking by pressing the START/STOP button.
7. Flip the shanks halfway through, and resume cooking.
8. Meanwhile, add and heat the remaining olive oil in a skillet.
9. Add onion and garlic to sauté for 5 minutes.
10. Add in mushrooms and cook for 5 minutes.
11. Add red wine and cook until it is absorbed
12. Stir all the remaining vegetables along with black pepper and salt.
13. Cook until vegetables are al dente.
14. Serve the air fried shanks with sautéed vegetable fry.

Nutrition Info:
- (Per serving) Calories 352 | Fat 9.1g | Sodium 1294mg | Carbs 3.9g | Fiber 1g | Sugar 1g | Protein 61g

Ninja Dual Zone Air Fryer Cookbook | 34

Pork Tenderloin With Brown Sugar–pecan Sweet Potatoes

Servings: 4
Cooking Time: 45 Minutes

Ingredients:
- FOR THE PORK TENDERLOIN
- 1½ pounds pork tenderloin
- 2 teaspoons vegetable oil
- ½ teaspoon kosher salt
- ½ teaspoon poultry seasoning
- FOR THE SWEET POTATOES
- 4 teaspoons unsalted butter, at room temperature
- 2 tablespoons dark brown sugar
- ¼ cup chopped pecans
- 4 small sweet potatoes

Directions:
1. To prep the pork: Coat the pork tenderloin with the oil, then rub with the salt and poultry seasoning.
2. To prep the sweet potatoes: In a small bowl, mix the butter, brown sugar, and pecans until well combined.
3. To cook the pork and sweet potatoes: Install a crisper plate in the Zone 1 basket. Place the pork tenderloin in the basket and insert the basket in the unit. Place the sweet potatoes in the Zone 2 basket and insert the basket in the unit.
4. Select Zone 1, select AIR FRY, set the temperature to 390°F, and set the time to 25 minutes.
5. Select Zone 2, select BAKE, set the temperature to 400°F, and set the time to 45 minutes. Select SMART FINISH.
6. Press START/PAUSE to begin cooking.
7. When the Zone 2 timer reads 10 minutes, press START/PAUSE. Remove the basket. Slice the sweet potatoes open lengthwise. Divide the pecan mixture among the potatoes. Reinsert the basket and press START/PAUSE to resume cooking.
8. When cooking is complete, the pork will be cooked through (an instant-read thermometer should read 145°F) and the potatoes will be soft and their flesh fluffy.
9. Transfer the pork loin to a plate or cutting board and let rest for at least 5 minutes before slicing and serving.

Nutrition Info:
- (Per serving) Calories: 415; Total fat: 15g; Saturated fat: 4.5g; Carbohydrates: 33g; Fiber: 4.5g; Protein: 36g; Sodium: 284mg

Mustard Rubbed Lamb Chops

Servings: 4
Cooking Time: 31 Minutes.

Ingredients:
- 1 teaspoon Dijon mustard
- 1 teaspoon olive oil
- ½ teaspoon soy sauce
- ½ teaspoon garlic, minced
- ½ teaspoon cumin powder
- ½ teaspoon cayenne pepper
- ½ teaspoon Italian spice blend
- ⅛ teaspoon salt
- 4 pieces of lamb chops

Directions:
1. Mix Dijon mustard, soy sauce, olive oil, garlic, cumin powder, cayenne pepper, Italian spice blend, and salt in a medium bowl and mix well.
2. Place lamb chops into a Ziploc bag and pour in the marinade.
3. Press the air out of the bag and seal tightly.
4. Press the marinade around the lamb chops to coat.
5. Keep then in the fridge and marinate for at least 30 minutes, up to overnight.
6. Place 2 chops in each of the crisper plate and spray them with cooking oil.
7. Return the crisper plate to the Ninja Foodi Dual Zone Air Fryer.
8. Select the Roast mode for Zone 1 and set the temperature to 350 degrees F and the time to 27 minutes.
9. Select the "MATCH" button to copy the settings for Zone 2.
10. Initiate cooking by pressing the START/STOP button.
11. Flip the chops once cooked halfway through, and resume cooking.
12. Switch the Roast mode to Max Crisp mode and cook for 5 minutes.
13. Serve warm.

Nutrition Info:
- (Per serving) Calories 264 | Fat 17g | Sodium 129mg | Carbs 0.9g | Fiber 0.3g | Sugar 0g | Protein 27g

Meatloaf

Servings: 6
Cooking Time: 25 Minutes

Ingredients:
- For the meatloaf:
- 2 pounds ground beef
- 2 eggs, beaten
- 2 cups old-fashioned oats, regular or gluten-free
- ½ cup evaporated milk
- ½ cup chopped onion
- ½ teaspoon garlic salt
- For the sauce:
- 1 cup ketchup
- ¾ cup brown sugar, packed
- ¼ cup chopped onion
- ½ teaspoon liquid smoke
- ¼ teaspoon garlic powder
- Olive oil cooking spray

Directions:
1. In a large bowl, combine all the meatloaf ingredients.
2. Spray 2 sheets of foil with olive oil cooking spray.
3. Form the meatloaf mixture into a loaf shape, cut in half, and place each half on one piece of foil.
4. Roll the foil up a bit on the sides. Allow it to be slightly open.
5. Put all the sauce ingredients in a saucepan and whisk until combined on medium-low heat. This should only take 1–2 minutes
6. Install a crisper plate in both drawers. Place half the meatloaf in the zone 1 drawer and half in zone 2's, then insert the drawers into the unit.
7. Select zone 1, select AIR FRY, set temperature to 390 degrees F/ 200 degrees C, and set time to 25 minutes. Select MATCH to match zone 2 settings to zone 1. Press the START/STOP button to begin cooking.
8. When the time reaches 20 minutes, press START/STOP to pause the unit. Remove the drawers and coat the meatloaf with the sauce using a brush. Re-insert the drawers into the unit and press START/STOP to resume cooking.
9. Carefully remove and serve.

Nutrition Info:
- (Per serving) Calories 727 | Fat 34g | Sodium 688mg | Carbs 57g | Fiber 3g | Sugar 34g | Protein 49g

Italian-style Meatballs With Garlicky Roasted Broccoli

Servings: 4
Cooking Time: 15 Minutes

Ingredients:
- FOR THE MEATBALLS
- 1 large egg
- ¼ cup Italian-style bread crumbs
- 1 pound ground beef (85 percent lean)
- ¼ cup grated Parmesan cheese
- ¼ teaspoon kosher salt
- Nonstick cooking spray
- 2 cups marinara sauce
- FOR THE ROASTED BROCCOLI
- 4 cups broccoli florets
- 1 tablespoon olive oil
- ¼ teaspoon kosher salt
- ¼ teaspoon freshly ground pepper
- ¼ teaspoon red pepper flakes
- 1 tablespoon minced garlic

Directions:
1. To prep the meatballs: In a large bowl, beat the egg. Mix in the bread crumbs and let sit for 5 minutes.
2. Add the beef, Parmesan, and salt and mix until just combined. Form the meatball mixture into 8 meatballs, about 1 inch in diameter. Mist with cooking spray.
3. To prep the broccoli: In a large bowl, combine the broccoli, olive oil, salt, black pepper, and red pepper flakes. Toss to coat the broccoli evenly.
4. To cook the meatballs and broccoli: Install a crisper plate in the Zone 1 basket. Place the meatballs in the basket and insert the basket in the unit. Place the broccoli in the Zone 2 basket, sprinkle the garlic over the broccoli, and insert the basket in the unit.
5. Select Zone 1, select AIR FRY, set the temperature to 400°F, and set the time to 12 minutes.
6. Select Zone 2, select ROAST, set the temperature to 390°F, and set the time to 15 minutes. Select SMART FINISH.
7. Press START/PAUSE to begin cooking.
8. When the Zone 1 timer reads 5 minutes, press START/PAUSE. Remove the basket and pour the marinara sauce over the meatballs. Reinsert the basket and press START/PAUSE to resume cooking.
9. When cooking is complete, the meatballs should be cooked through and the broccoli will have begun to brown on the edges.

Nutrition Info:
- (Per serving) Calories: 493; Total fat: 33g; Saturated fat: 9g; Carbohydrates: 24g; Fiber: 3g; Protein: 31g; Sodium: 926mg

Air Fried Lamb Chops

Servings: 4
Cooking Time: 10 Minutes

Ingredients:
- 700g lamb chops
- ½ teaspoon oregano
- 3 tablespoons parsley, minced
- ½ teaspoon black pepper
- 3 cloves garlic minced
- 2 tablespoons lemon juice
- 2 tablespoons olive oil
- Salt to taste

Directions:
1. Pat dry the chops and mix with lemon juice and the rest of the ingredients.
2. Place these chops in the air fryer baskets.
3. Return the air fryer basket 1 to Zone 1, and basket 2 to Zone 2 of the Ninja Foodi 2-Basket Air Fryer.
4. Choose the "Air Fry" mode for Zone 1and set the temperature to 400 degrees F and 10 minutes of cooking time.
5. Select the "MATCH COOK" option to copy the settings for Zone 2.
6. Initiate cooking by pressing the START/PAUSE BUTTON.
7. Flip the pork chops once cooked halfway through.
8. Serve warm.

Nutrition Info:
- (Per serving) Calories 396 | Fat 23.2g |Sodium 622mg | Carbs 0.7g | Fiber 0g | Sugar 0g | Protein 45.6g

Lamb Chops With Dijon Garlic

Servings: 4
Cooking Time: 22 Minutes

Ingredients:
- 2 teaspoons Dijon mustard
- 2 teaspoons olive oil
- 1 teaspoon soy sauce
- 1 teaspoon garlic, minced
- 1 teaspoon cumin powder
- 1 teaspoon cayenne pepper
- 1 teaspoon Italian spice blend (optional)
- ¼ teaspoon salt
- 8 lamb chops

Directions:
1. Combine the Dijon mustard, olive oil, soy sauce, garlic, cumin powder, cayenne pepper, Italian spice blend (optional), and salt in a medium mixing bowl.
2. Put the marinade in a large Ziploc bag. Add the lamb chops. Seal the bag tightly after pressing out the air. Coat the lamb in the marinade by shaking the bag and pressing the chops into the mixture. Place in the fridge for at least 30 minutes, or up to overnight, to marinate.
3. Install a crisper plate in both drawers. Place half the lamb chops in the zone 1 drawer and half in zone 2's, then insert the drawers into the unit.
4. Select zone 1, select AIR FRY, set temperature to 390 degrees F/ 200 degrees C, and set time to 22 minutes. Select MATCH to match zone 2 settings to zone 1. Press the START/STOP button to begin cooking.
5. When the time reaches 11 minutes, press START/STOP to pause the unit. Remove the drawers and flip the lamb chops. Re-insert the drawers into the unit and press START/STOP to resume cooking.
6. Serve and enjoy!

Nutrition Info:
- (Per serving) Calories 343 | Fat 15.1g | Sodium 380mg | Carbs 0.9 g | Fiber 0.3g | Sugar 0.1g | Protein 48.9g

Steak And Mashed Creamy Potatoes

Servings: 1
Cooking Time: 45

Ingredients:
- 2 Russet potatoes, peeled and cubed
- ¼ cup butter, divided
- 1/3 cup heavy cream
- ½ cup shredded cheddar cheese
- Salt and black pepper, to taste
- 1 New York strip steak, about a pound
- 1 teaspoon of olive oil
- Oil spray, for greasing

Directions:
1. Rub the potatoes with salt and a little amount of olive oil about a teaspoon.
2. Next, season the steak with salt and black pepper.
3. Place the russet potatoes in a zone 1 basket.
4. Oil spray the steak from both sides and then place it in the zone 2 basket.
5. Set zone 1 to AIR fry mode for 45 minutes at 390 degrees F.
6. Set the zone 2 basket, at 12 minutes at 375 degrees F.
7. Hot start and Lethe ninja foodie do its magic.
8. One the cooking cycle completes, take out the steak and potatoes.
9. Mash the potatoes and then add butter, heavy cream, and cheese along with salt and black pepper.
10. Serve the mashed potatoes with steak.
11. Enjoy.

Nutrition Info:
- (Per serving) Calories1932 | Fat 85.2g| Sodium 3069mg | Carbs 82g | Fiber10.3 g| Sugar 5.3g | Protein 22.5g

Beef & Broccoli

Servings: 4
Cooking Time: 12

Ingredients:
- 12 ounces of teriyaki sauce, divided
- ½ tablespoon garlic powder
- ¼ cup of soy sauce
- 1 pound raw sirloin steak, thinly sliced
- 2 cups broccoli, cut into florets
- 2 teaspoons of olive oil
- Salt and black pepper, to taste

Directions:
1. Take a zip-lock plastic bag and mix teriyaki sauce, salt, garlic powder, black pepper, soy sauce, and olive oil.
2. Marinate the beef in it for 2 hours.
3. Then drain the beef from the marinade.
4. Now toss the broccoli with oil, teriyaki sauce, and salt and black pepper.
5. Put it in a zone 1 basket
6. Now for the zone, 1 basket set it to AIRFRY mode at 400 degrees F for 15 minutes.
7. Place the steak in a zone 2 basket and set it to AIR FRY mode at 375 degrees F for 10-12 minutes.
8. Hit start and let the cooking cycle completes.
9. Once it's done take out the beef and broccoli and
10. serve immediately with leftover teriyaki sauce and cooked rice.

Nutrition Info:
- (Per serving) Calories 344| Fat 10g| Sodium 4285mg | Carbs18.2 g | Fiber 1.5g| Sugar 13.3g | Protein42 g

Korean Bbq Beef

Servings: 6
Cooking Time: 30 Minutes

Ingredients:
- For the meat:
- 1 pound flank steak or thinly sliced steak
- ¼ cup corn starch
- Coconut oil spray
- For the sauce:
- ½ cup soy sauce or gluten-free soy sauce
- ½ cup brown sugar
- 2 tablespoons white wine vinegar
- 1 clove garlic, crushed
- 1 tablespoon hot chili sauce
- 1 teaspoon ground ginger
- ½ teaspoon sesame seeds
- 1 tablespoon corn starch
- 1 tablespoon water

Directions:
1. To begin, prepare the steak. Thinly slice it in that toss it in the corn starch to be coated thoroughly. Spray the tops with some coconut oil.
2. Spray the crisping plates and drawers with the coconut oil.
3. Place the crisping plates into the drawers. Place the steak strips into each drawer. Insert both drawers into the unit.
4. Select zone 1, Select AIR FRY, set the temperature to 375 degrees F/ 190 degrees C, and set time to 30 minutes. Select MATCH to match zone 2 settings with zone 1. Press the START/STOP button to begin cooking.
5. While the steak is cooking, add the sauce ingredients EXCEPT for the corn starch and water to a medium saucepan.
6. Warm it up to a low boil, then whisk in the corn starch and water.
7. Carefully remove the steak and pour the sauce over. Mix well.

Nutrition Info:
- (Per serving) Calories 500 | Fat 19.8g | Sodium 680mg | Carbs 50.1g | Fiber 4.1g | Sugar 0g | Protein 27.9g

Juicy Pork Chops

Servings: 4
Cooking Time: 15 Minutes

Ingredients:
- 450g pork chops
- ¼ tsp garlic powder
- 15ml olive oil
- ¼ tsp smoked paprika
- Pepper
- Salt

Directions:
1. In a small bowl, mix the garlic powder, paprika, pepper, and salt.
2. Brush the pork chops with oil and rub with spice mixture.
3. Insert a crisper plate in the Ninja Foodi air fryer baskets.
4. Place the pork chops in both baskets.
5. Select zone 1, then select "bake" mode and set the temperature to 410 degrees F for 15 minutes. Press "match" to match zone 2 settings to zone 1. Press "start/stop" to begin. Turn halfway through.

Nutrition Info:
- (Per serving) Calories 394 | Fat 31.7g | Sodium 118mg | Carbs 0.2g | Fiber 0.1g | Sugar 0.1g | Protein 25.5g

Recipe

From the kicthen of ....

Serves .... Prep time .... Cook time ....

☐ Difficulty   ☐ Easy   ☐ Medium   ☐ Hard

Ingredient

Directions

POULTRY RECIPES

Almond Chicken 47

Bacon-wrapped Chicken 44

Chicken Cordon Bleu 45

Chili Chicken Wings 46

Cornish Hen With Asparagus 45

Delicious Chicken Skewers 42

Dijon Chicken Wings 43

Garlic, Buffalo, And Blue Cheese Stuffed Chicken 44

Glazed Thighs With French Fries 46

Honey Butter Chicken 43

Italian Chicken & Potatoes 42

Thai Chicken Meatballs 48

Turkey Meatloaf With Veggie Medley 48

Veggie Stuffed Chicken Breasts 47

Poultry Recipes

Delicious Chicken Skewers

Servings: 4
Cooking Time: 15 Minutes

Ingredients:
- 900g chicken thighs, cut into cubes
- 45ml fresh lime juice
- 59ml coconut milk
- 2 tbsp Thai red curry
- 35ml maple syrup
- 120ml tamari soy sauce

Directions:
1. Add chicken and remaining ingredients into the bowl and mix well.
2. Cover the bowl and place in the refrigerator for 2 hours.
3. Thread the marinated chicken onto the soaked skewers.
4. Insert a crisper plate in the Ninja Foodi air fryer baskets.
5. Place the chicken skewers in both baskets.
6. Select zone 1 then select "air fry" mode and set the temperature to 360 degrees F for 15 minutes. Press "match" to match zone 2 settings to zone 1. Press "start/stop" to begin.

Nutrition Info:
- (Per serving) Calories 526 | Fat 20.5g | Sodium 2210mg | Carbs 12.9g | Fiber 0.6g | Sugar 10g | Protein 69.7g

Italian Chicken & Potatoes

Servings: 4
Cooking Time: 24 Minutes

Ingredients:
- 450g chicken breast, boneless & diced
- 30ml olive oil
- ½ tsp lemon zest
- 2 tbsp fresh lemon juice
- 450g baby potatoes, quartered
- 1 tbsp Greek seasoning
- Pepper
- Salt

Directions:
1. Toss potatoes with ½ tablespoon Greek seasoning, 1 tablespoon oil, lemon zest, lemon juice, pepper, and salt in a bowl.
2. Insert a crisper plate in the Ninja Foodi air fryer baskets.
3. Add potatoes into the zone 1 basket.
4. In a bowl, toss chicken with the remaining oil and seasoning.
5. Add the chicken into the zone 2 basket.
6. Select zone 1, then select "air fry" mode and set the temperature to 390 degrees F for 12 minutes. Press "match" to match zone 2 settings to zone 1. Press "start/stop" to begin.

Nutrition Info:
- (Per serving) Calories 262 | Fat 10.1g | Sodium 227mg | Carbs 15.5g | Fiber 2.9g | Sugar 0.2g | Protein 27.2g

Honey Butter Chicken

Servings: 4
Cooking Time: 15 Minutes

Ingredients:
- 4 chicken breasts, boneless
- 85g honey
- 28g butter, melted
- 2 tsp lemon juice
- 15ml olive oil
- 62g Dijon mustard
- Pepper
- Salt

Directions:
1. In a small bowl, mix butter, oil, lemon juice, honey, mustard, pepper, and salt.
2. Insert a crisper plate in the Ninja Foodi air fryer baskets.
3. Brush chicken breasts with butter mixture and place them in both baskets.
4. Select zone 1 then select "bake" mode and set the temperature to 380 degrees F for 15 minutes. Press "match" to match zone 2 settings to zone 1. Press "start/stop" to begin.

Nutrition Info:
- (Per serving) Calories 434 | Fat 20.7g | Sodium 384mg | Carbs 18.4g | Fiber 0.6g | Sugar 17.6g | Protein 43.1g

Dijon Chicken Wings

Servings: 3
Cooking Time: 20 Minutes

Ingredients:
- 1 cup chicken batter mix, Louisiana
- 9 chicken wings
- ½ teaspoon smoked Paprika
- 2 tablespoons Dijon mustard
- 1 tablespoon cayenne pepper
- 1 teaspoon meat tenderizer, powder
- Oil spray, for greasing

Directions:
1. Pat dry the chicken wings and add mustard, paprika, meat tenderizer, and cayenne pepper.
2. Dredge the wings in the chicken batter mix.
3. Oil spray the chicken wings.
4. Grease both baskets of the air fryer.
5. Divide the wings between the two zones of the air fryer.
6. Set zone 1 to AIR FRY mode at 400 degrees F/ 200 degrees C for 20 minutes.
7. Select MATCH for zone 2.
8. Hit START/STOP button to begin the cooking.
9. Once the cooking cycle is complete, serve, and enjoy hot.

Nutrition Info:
- (Per serving) Calories 621 | Fat 32.6g | Sodium 2016mg | Carbs 46.6g | Fiber 1.1g | Sugar 0.2g | Protein 32.1g

Garlic, Buffalo, And Blue Cheese Stuffed Chicken

Servings: 2
Cooking Time: 30 Minutes

Ingredients:
- ¼ teaspoon garlic powder
- ¼ teaspoon onion powder
- ¼ teaspoon paprika
- 2 boneless, skinless chicken breasts
- ½ tablespoon canola oil
- 2 ounces softened cream cheese
- ¼ cup shredded cheddar cheese
- ¼ cup blue cheese crumbles
- ¼ cup buffalo sauce
- 1 tablespoon dry ranch seasoning
- 2 tablespoons dried chives
- 1 tablespoon minced garlic
- Optional toppings:
- Ranch dressing
- Buffalo sauce
- Fresh parsley

Directions:
1. Combine the garlic powder, onion powder, and paprika in a small bowl.
2. Drizzle the chicken breasts with oil and season evenly with the garlic powder mixture on a cutting board.
3. Make a deep pocket in the center of each chicken breast, but be cautious not to cut all the way through.
4. Combine the remaining ingredients in a medium mixing bowl and stir until thoroughly blended. Fill each chicken breast's pocket with the cream cheese mixture.
5. Place the chicken in both drawers and insert both drawers into the unit. Select zone 1, then BAKE, and set the temperature to 375 degrees F/ 190 degrees C with a 30-minute timer. To match zone 2 and zone 1 settings, select MATCH. To start cooking, use the START/STOP button.
6. Garnish the cooked chicken with ranch dressing, spicy sauce, and parsley on top.

Nutrition Info:
- (Per serving) Calories 369 | Fat 23.8g | Sodium 568mg | Carbs 4.3g | Fiber 0.4g | Sugar 0.5g | Protein 34.7g

Bacon-wrapped Chicken

Servings: 2
Cooking Time: 28 Minutes.

Ingredients:
- Butter:
- ½ stick butter softened
- ½ garlic clove, minced
- ¼ teaspoon dried thyme
- ¼ teaspoon dried basil
- ⅛ teaspoon coarse salt
- 1 pinch black pepper, ground
- ⅓ lb. thick-cut bacon
- 1 ½ lbs. boneless skinless chicken thighs
- 2 teaspoons garlic, minced

Directions:
1. Mix garlic softened butter with thyme, salt, basil, and black pepper in a bowl.
2. Add butter mixture on a piece of wax paper and roll it up tightly to make a butter log.
3. Place the log in the refrigerator for 2 hours.
4. Spray one bacon strip on a piece of wax paper.
5. Place each chicken thigh on top of one bacon strip and rub it with garlic.
6. Make a slit in the chicken thigh and add a teaspoon of butter to the chicken.
7. Wrap the bacon around the chicken thigh.
8. Repeat those same steps with all the chicken thighs.
9. Place the bacon-wrapped chicken thighs in the two crisper plates.
10. Return the crisper plates to the Ninja Foodi Dual Zone Air Fryer.
11. Choose the Air Fry mode for Zone 1 and set the temperature to 390 degrees F and the time to 28 minutes.
12. Select the "MATCH" button to copy the settings for Zone 2.
13. Initiate cooking by pressing the START/STOP button.
14. Flip the chicken once cooked halfway through, and resume cooking.
15. Serve warm.

Nutrition Info:
- (Per serving) Calories 380 | Fat 29g | Sodium 821mg | Carbs 34.6g | Fiber 0g | Sugar 0g | Protein 30g

Cornish Hen With Asparagus

Servings: 2
Cooking Time: 45

Ingredients:
- 10 spears of asparagus
- Salt and black pepper, to taste
- 1 Cornish hen
- Salt, to taste
- Black pepper, to taste
- 1 teaspoon of Paprika
- Coconut spray, for greasing
- 2 lemons, sliced

Directions:
1. Wash and pat dry the asparagus and coat it with coconut oil spray.
2. Sprinkle salt on the asparagus and place inside the first basket of the air fryer.
3. Next, take the Cornish hen and rub it well with the salt, black pepper, and paprika.
4. Oil sprays the Cornish hen and place in the second air fryer basket.
5. Press button 1 for the first basket and set it to AIR FRY mode at 350 degrees F, for 8 minutes.
6. For the second basket hit 2 and set the time to 45 minutes at 350 degrees F, by selecting the ROAST mode.
7. To start cooking, hit the smart finish button and press hit start.
8. Once the 6 minutes pass press 1 and pause and take out the asparagus.
9. Once the chicken cooking cycle complete, press 2 and hit pause.
10. Take out the Basket of chicken and let it transfer to the serving plate
11. Serve the chicken with roasted asparagus and slices of lemon.
12. Serve hot and enjoy.

Nutrition Info:
- (Per serving) Calories 192| Fat 4.7g| Sodium 151mg | Carbs10.7 g | Fiber 4.6g | Sugar 3.8g | Protein 30g

Chicken Cordon Bleu

Servings: 4
Cooking Time: 20 Minutes

Ingredients:
- 4 boneless, skinless chicken breast halves (4 ounces each)
- ¼ teaspoon salt
- ¼ teaspoon pepper
- 4 slices deli ham
- 2 slices aged Swiss cheese, halved
- 1 cup panko breadcrumbs
- Cooking spray
- For the sauce:
- 1 tablespoon all-purpose flour
- ½ cup 2% milk
- ¼ cup dry white wine
- 3 tablespoons finely shredded Swiss cheese
- 1/8 teaspoon salt
- Dash pepper

Directions:
1. Season both sides of the chicken breast halves with salt and pepper. You may need to thin the breasts with a mallet.
2. Place 1 slice of ham and half slice of cheese on top of each chicken breast half.
3. Roll the breast up and use toothpicks to secure it.
4. Sprinkle the breadcrumbs on top and spray lightly with the cooking oil.
5. Insert a crisper plate into each drawer. Divide the chicken between each drawer and insert the drawers into the unit.
6. Select zone 1, select AIR FRY, set temperature to 390 degrees F/ 200 degrees C, and set time to 7 minutes. Select MATCH to match zone 2 settings to zone 1. Press the START/STOP button to begin cooking.
7. When the time reaches 5 minutes, press START/STOP to pause the unit. Remove the drawers and flip the chicken. Re-insert the drawers into the unit and press START/STOP to resume cooking.
8. To make the sauce, mix the flour, wine, and milk together in a small pot until smooth. Bring to a boil over high heat, stirring frequently, for 1–2 minutes, or until the sauce has thickened.
9. Reduce the heat to medium. Add the cheese. Cook and stir for 2–3 minutes, or until the cheese has melted and the sauce has thickened and bubbled. Add salt and pepper to taste. Keep the sauce heated at a low temperature until ready to serve.

Nutrition Info:
- (Per serving) Calories 272 | Fat 8g | Sodium 519mg | Carbs 14g | Fiber 2g | Sugar 1g | Protein 32g

Glazed Thighs With French Fries

Servings: 3
Cooking Time: 35

Ingredients:
- 2 tablespoons of Soy Sauce
- Salt, to taste
- 1 teaspoon of Worcestershire Sauce
- 2 teaspoons Brown Sugar
- 1 teaspoon of Ginger, paste
- 1 teaspoon of Garlic, paste
- 6 Boneless Chicken Thighs
- 1 pound of hand-cut potato fries
- 2 tablespoons of canola oil

Directions:
1. Coat the French fries well with canola oil.
2. Season it with salt.
3. In a small bowl, combine the soy sauce, Worcestershire sauce, brown sugar, ginger, and garlic.
4. Place the chicken in this marinade and let it sit for 40 minutes.
5. Put the chicken thighs into the zone 1 basket and fries into the zone 2 basket.
6. Press button 1 for the first basket, and set it to ROAST mode at 350 degrees F for 35 minutes.
7. For the second basket hit 2 and set time to 30 minutes at 360 degrees F, by selecting AIR FRY mode.
8. Once the cooking cycle completely take out the fries and chicken and serve it hot.

Nutrition Info:
- (Per serving) Calories 858| Fat39g | Sodium 1509mg | Carbs 45.6g | Fiber 4.4g | Sugar3 g | Protein 90g

Chili Chicken Wings

Servings: 4
Cooking Time: 43 Minutes.

Ingredients:
- 8 chicken wings drumettes
- cooking spray
- ⅛ cup low-fat buttermilk
- ¼ cup almond flour
- McCormick Chicken Seasoning to taste
- Thai Chili Marinade
- 1 ½ tablespoons low-sodium soy sauce
- ½ teaspoon ginger, minced
- 1 ½ garlic cloves
- 1 green onion
- ½ teaspoon rice wine vinegar
- ½ tablespoon Sriracha sauce
- ½ tablespoon sesame oil

Directions:
1. Put all the ingredients for the marinade in the blender and blend them for 1 minute.
2. Keep this marinade aside. Pat dry the washed chicken and place it in the Ziploc bag.
3. Add buttermilk, chicken seasoning, and zip the bag.
4. Shake the bag well, then refrigerator for 30 minutes for marination.
5. Remove the chicken drumettes from the marinade, then dredge them through dry flour.
6. Spread the drumettes in the two crisper plate and spray them with cooking oil.
7. Return the crisper plate to the Ninja Foodi Dual Zone Air Fryer.
8. Choose the Air Fry mode for Zone 1 and set the temperature to 390 degrees F and the time to 43 minutes.
9. Select the "MATCH" button to copy the settings for Zone 2.
10. Initiate cooking by pressing the START/STOP button.
11. Toss the drumettes once cooked halfway through.
12. Now brush the chicken pieces with Thai chili sauce and then resume cooking.
13. Serve warm.

Nutrition Info:
- (Per serving) Calories 223 | Fat 11.7g |Sodium 721mg | Carbs 13.6g | Fiber 0.7g | Sugar 8g | Protein 15.7g

Almond Chicken

Servings: 4
Cooking Time: 25 Minutes

Ingredients:
- 2 large eggs
- ½ cup buttermilk
- 2 teaspoons garlic salt
- 1 teaspoon pepper
- 2 cups slivered almonds, finely chopped
- 4 boneless, skinless chicken breast halves (6 ounces each)

Directions:
1. Whisk together the egg, buttermilk, garlic salt, and pepper in a small bowl.
2. In another small bowl, place the almonds.
3. Dip the chicken in the egg mixture, then roll it in the almonds, patting it down to help the coating stick.
4. Install a crisper plate in both drawers. Place half the chicken breasts in the zone 1 drawer and half in zone 2's, then insert the drawers into the unit.
5. Select zone 1, select AIR FRY, set temperature to 390 degrees F/ 200 degrees C, and set time to 22 minutes. Select MATCH to match zone 2 settings to zone 1. Press the START/STOP button to begin cooking.
6. When the time reaches 11 minutes, press START/STOP to pause the unit. Remove the drawers and flip the chicken. Re-insert the drawers into the unit and press START/STOP to resume cooking.
7. When cooking is complete, remove the chicken.

Nutrition Info:
- (Per serving) Calories 353 | Fat 18g | Sodium 230mg | Carbs 6g | Fiber 2g | Sugar 3g | Protein 41g

Veggie Stuffed Chicken Breasts

Servings: 2
Cooking Time: 10 Minutes.

Ingredients:
- 4 teaspoons chili powder
- 4 teaspoons ground cumin
- 1 skinless, boneless chicken breast
- 2 teaspoons chipotle flakes
- 2 teaspoons Mexican oregano
- Salt and black pepper, to taste
- ½ red bell pepper, julienned
- ½ onion, julienned
- 1 fresh jalapeno pepper, julienned
- 2 teaspoons corn oil
- ½ lime, juiced

Directions:
1. Slice the chicken breast in half horizontally.
2. Pound each chicken breast with a mallet into ¼ inch thickness.
3. Rub the pounded chicken breast with black pepper, salt, oregano, chipotle flakes, cumin, and chili powder.
4. Add ½ of bell pepper, jalapeno, and onion on top of each chicken breast piece.
5. Roll the chicken to wrap the filling inside and insert toothpicks to seal.
6. Place the rolls in crisper plate and spray them with cooking oil.
7. Return the crisper plate to the Ninja Foodi Dual Zone Air Fryer.
8. Choose the Air Fry mode for Zone 1 and set the temperature to 360 degrees F and the time to 10 minutes.
9. Initiate cooking by pressing the START/STOP button.
10. Serve warm.

Nutrition Info:
- (Per serving) Calories 351 | Fat 11g | Sodium 150mg | Carbs 3.3g | Fiber 0.2g | Sugar 1g | Protein 33.2g

Thai Chicken Meatballs

Servings: 4
Cooking Time: 10 Minutes

Ingredients:
- ½ cup sweet chili sauce
- 2 tablespoons lime juice
- 2 tablespoons ketchup
- 1 teaspoon soy sauce
- 1 large egg, lightly beaten
- ¾ cup panko breadcrumbs
- 1 green onion, finely chopped
- 1 tablespoon minced fresh cilantro
- ½ teaspoon salt
- ½ teaspoon garlic powder
- 1-pound lean ground chicken

Directions:
1. Combine the chili sauce, lime juice, ketchup, and soy sauce in a small bowl; set aside ½ cup for serving.
2. Combine the egg, breadcrumbs, green onion, cilantro, salt, garlic powder, and the remaining 4 tablespoons chili sauce mixture in a large mixing bowl. Mix in the chicken lightly yet thoroughly. Form into 12 balls.
3. Install a crisper plate in both drawers. Place half the chicken meatballs in the zone 1 drawer and half in zone 2's, then insert the drawers into the unit.
4. Select zone 1, select AIR FRY, set temperature to 390 degrees F/ 200 degrees C, and set time to 10 minutes. Select MATCH to match zone 2 settings to zone 1. Press the START/STOP button to begin cooking.
5. When the time reaches 5 minutes, press START/STOP to pause the unit. Remove the drawers and flip the chicken. Re-insert the drawers into the unit and press START/STOP to resume cooking.
6. When cooking is complete, remove the chicken meatballs and serve hot.

Nutrition Info:
- (Per serving) Calories 93 | Fat 3g | Sodium 369mg | Carbs 9g | Fiber 0g | Sugar 6g | Protein 9g

Turkey Meatloaf With Veggie Medley

Servings: 4
Cooking Time: 30 Minutes

Ingredients:
- FOR THE MEATLOAF
- 1 large egg
- ¼ cup ketchup
- 2 teaspoons Worcestershire sauce
- ½ cup Italian-style bread crumbs
- 1 teaspoon kosher salt
- 1 pound ground turkey (93 percent lean)
- 1 tablespoon vegetable oil
- FOR THE VEGGIE MEDLEY
- 2 carrots, thinly sliced
- 8 ounces green beans, trimmed (about 2 cups)
- 2 cups broccoli florets
- 1 red bell pepper, sliced into strips
- 2 tablespoons vegetable oil
- ½ teaspoon kosher salt
- ½ teaspoon freshly ground black pepper

Directions:
1. To prep the meatloaf: In a large bowl, whisk the egg. Stir in the ketchup, Worcestershire sauce, bread crumbs, and salt. Let sit for 5 minutes to allow the bread crumbs to absorb some moisture.
2. Gently mix in the turkey until just incorporated. Form the mixture into a loaf. Brush with the oil.
3. To prep the veggie medley: In a large bowl, combine the carrots, green beans, broccoli, bell pepper, oil, salt, and black pepper. Mix well to coat the vegetables with the oil.
4. To cook the meatloaf and veggie medley: Install a crisper plate in each of the two baskets. Place the meatloaf in the Zone 1 basket and insert the basket in the unit. Place the vegetables in the Zone 2 basket and insert the basket in the unit.
5. Select Zone 1, select ROAST, set the temperature to 350°F, and set the time to 30 minutes.
6. Select Zone 2, select AIR FRY, set the temperature to 390°F, and set the time to 20 minutes. Select SMART FINISH.
7. Press START/PAUSE to begin cooking.
8. When cooking is complete, the meatloaf will be cooked through (an instant-read thermometer should read 165°F) and the vegetables will be tender and roasted.

Nutrition Info:
- (Per serving) Calories: 394; Total fat: 20g; Saturated fat: 4.5g; Carbohydrates: 25g; Fiber: 4.5g; Protein: 28g; Sodium: 952mg

Fish And Seafood Recipes

Bang Bang Shrimp 56

Chili Lime Tilapia 51

Codfish With Herb Vinaigrette 55

Crispy Parmesan Cod 53

Delicious Haddock 52

Fried Lobster Tails 51

"fried" Fish With Seasoned Potato Wedges 52

Roasted Salmon And Parmesan Asparagus 56

Salmon With Green Beans 55

Scallops With Greens 50

Smoked Salmon 53

Spicy Fish Fillet With Onion Rings 54

Spicy Salmon Fillets 50

Two-way Salmon 54

Fish And Seafood Recipes

Scallops With Greens

Servings: 8
Cooking Time: 13 Minutes.

Ingredients:
- ¾ cup heavy whipping cream
- 1 tablespoon tomato paste
- 1 tablespoon chopped fresh basil
- 1 teaspoon garlic, minced
- ½ teaspoons salt
- ½ teaspoons pepper
- 12 ounces frozen spinach thawed
- 8 jumbo sea scallops
- Vegetable oil to spray

Directions:
1. Season the scallops with vegetable oil, salt, and pepper in a bowl
2. Mix cream with spinach, basil, garlic, salt, pepper, and tomato paste in a bowl.
3. Pour this mixture over the scallops and mix gently.
4. Divide the scallops in the Air Fryers Baskets without using the crisper plate.
5. Return the crisper plate to the Ninja Foodi Dual Zone Air Fryer.
6. Choose the Air Fry mode for Zone 1 and set the temperature to 390 degrees F and the time to 13 minutes.
7. Select the "MATCH" button to copy the settings for Zone 2.
8. Initiate cooking by pressing the START/STOP button.
9. Serve right away

Nutrition Info:
- (Per serving) Calories 266 | Fat 6.3g |Sodium 193mg | Carbs 39.1g | Fiber 7.2g | Sugar 5.2g | Protein 14.8g

Spicy Salmon Fillets

Servings: 6
Cooking Time: 8 Minutes

Ingredients:
- 900g salmon fillets
- ¾ tsp ground cumin
- 1 tbsp brown sugar
- 2 tbsp steak seasoning
- ¼ tsp cayenne pepper
- ½ tsp ground coriander

Directions:
1. Mix ground cumin, coriander, steak seasoning, brown sugar, and cayenne in a small bowl.
2. Rub salmon fillets with spice mixture.
3. Insert a crisper plate in the Ninja Foodi air fryer baskets.
4. Place the salmon fillets in both baskets.
5. Select zone 1, then select "bake" mode and set the temperature to 360 degrees F for 10 minutes. Press "match" to match zone 2 settings to zone 1. Press "start/stop" to begin.

Nutrition Info:
- (Per serving) Calories 207 | Fat 9.4g |Sodium 68mg | Carbs 1.6g | Fiber 0.1g | Sugar 1.5g | Protein 29.4g

Chili Lime Tilapia

Servings: 4
Cooking Time: 10 Minutes

Ingredients:
- 340g tilapia fillets
- 2 teaspoons chili powder
- 1 teaspoon cumin
- 1 teaspoon garlic powder
- ½ teaspoon oregano
- ½ teaspoon sea salt
- ¼ teaspoon black pepper
- Lime zest from 1 lime
- Juice of ½ lime

Directions:
1. Mix chili powder and other spices with lime juice and zest in a bowl.
2. Rub this spice mixture over the tilapia fillets.
3. Place two fillets in each air basket.
4. Return the air fryer basket to the Ninja Foodi 2 Baskets Air Fryer.
5. Choose the "Air Fry" mode for Zone 1 at 400 degrees F and 10 minutes of cooking time.
6. Select the "MATCH COOK" option to copy the settings for Zone 2.
7. Initiate cooking by pressing the START/PAUSE BUTTON.
8. Flip the tilapia fillets once cooked halfway through.
9. Serve warm.

Nutrition Info:
- (Per serving) Calories 275 | Fat 1.4g | Sodium 582mg | Carbs 31.5g | Fiber 1.1g | Sugar 0.1g | Protein 29.8g

Fried Lobster Tails

Servings: 4
Cooking Time: 18 Minutes.

Ingredients:
- 4 (4-oz) lobster tails
- 8 tablespoons butter, melted
- 2 teaspoons lemon zest
- 2 garlic cloves, grated
- Salt and black pepper, ground to taste
- 2 teaspoons fresh parsley, chopped
- 4 wedges lemon

Directions:
1. Spread the lobster tails into Butterfly, slit the top to expose the lobster meat while keeping the tail intact.
2. Place two lobster tails in each of the crisper plate with their lobster meat facing up.
3. Mix melted butter with lemon zest and garlic in a bowl.
4. Brush the butter mixture on top of the lobster tails.
5. And drizzle salt and black pepper on top.
6. Return the crisper plate to the Ninja Foodi Dual Zone Air Fryer.
7. Choose the Air Fry mode for Zone 1 and set the temperature to 390 degrees F and the time to 18 minutes.
8. Select the "MATCH" button to copy the settings for Zone 2.
9. Initiate cooking by pressing the START/STOP button.
10. Garnish with parsley and lemon wedges.
11. Serve warm.

Nutrition Info:
- (Per serving) Calories 257 | Fat 10.4g | Sodium 431mg | Carbs 20g | Fiber 0g | Sugar 1.6g | Protein 21g

51 | Ninja Dual Zone Air Fryer Cookbook

"fried" Fish With Seasoned Potato Wedges

Servings: 4
Cooking Time: 30 Minutes

Ingredients:
- FOR THE FISH
- 4 cod fillets (6 ounces each)
- 4 tablespoons all-purpose flour, divided
- ¼ cup cornstarch
- 1 teaspoon baking powder
- ¼ teaspoon kosher salt
- ⅓ cup lager-style beer or sparkling water
- Tartar sauce, cocktail sauce, or malt vinegar, for serving (optional)
- FOR THE POTATOES
- 4 russet potatoes
- 2 tablespoons vegetable oil
- ½ teaspoon paprika
- ½ teaspoon kosher salt
- ¼ teaspoon garlic powder
- ¼ teaspoon freshly ground black pepper

Directions:
1. To prep the fish: Pat the fish dry with a paper towel and coat lightly with 2 tablespoons of flour.
2. In a shallow dish, combine the remaining 2 tablespoons of flour, the cornstarch, baking powder, and salt. Stir in the beer to form a thick batter.
3. Dip the fish in the batter to coat both sides, then let rest on a cutting board for 10 minutes.
4. To prep the potatoes: Cut each potato in half lengthwise, then cut each half into 4 wedges.
5. In a large bowl, combine the potatoes and oil. Toss well to fully coat the potatoes. Add the paprika, salt, garlic powder, and black pepper and toss well to coat.
6. To cook the fish and potato wedges: Install a crisper plate in each of the two baskets. Place a piece of parchment paper or aluminum foil over the plate in the Zone 1 basket. Place the fish in the basket and insert the basket in the unit. Place the potato wedges in a single layer in the Zone 2 basket and insert the basket in the unit.
7. Select Zone 1, select AIR FRY, set the temperature to 400°F, and set the timer to 13 minutes.
8. Select Zone 2, select AIR FRY, set the temperature to 400°F, and set the timer to 30 minutes. Select SMART FINISH.
9. Press START/PAUSE to begin cooking.
10. When the Zone 1 timer reads 5 minutes, press START/PAUSE. Remove the basket and use a silicone spatula to carefully flip the fish over. Reinsert the basket and press START/PAUSE to resume cooking.
11. When cooking is complete, the fish should be cooked through and the potatoes crispy outside and tender inside.

Serve hot with tartar sauce, cocktail sauce, or malt vinegar (if using).

Nutrition Info:
- (Per serving) Calories: 360; Total fat: 8g; Saturated fat: 1g; Carbohydrates: 40g; Fiber: 2g; Protein: 30g; Sodium: 302mg

Delicious Haddock

Servings: 4
Cooking Time: 10 Minutes

Ingredients:
- 1 egg
- 455g haddock fillets
- 1 tsp seafood seasoning
- 136g flour
- 15ml olive oil
- 119g breadcrumbs
- Pepper
- Salt

Directions:
1. In a shallow dish, whisk egg. Add flour to a plate.
2. In a separate shallow dish, mix breadcrumbs, pepper, seafood seasoning, and salt.
3. Brush fish fillets with oil.
4. Coat each fish fillet with flour, then dip in egg and finally coat with breadcrumbs.
5. Insert a crisper plate in the Ninja Foodi air fryer baskets.
6. Place coated fish fillets in both baskets.
7. Select zone 1, then select "air fry" mode and set the temperature to 360 degrees F for 10 minutes. Press "match" to match zone 2 settings to zone 1. Press "start/stop" to begin.

Nutrition Info:
- (Per serving) Calories 393 | Fat 7.4g | Sodium 351mg | Carbs 43.4g | Fiber 2.1g | Sugar 1.8g | Protein 35.7g

Crispy Parmesan Cod

Servings: 2
Cooking Time: 10 Minutes

Ingredients:
- 455g cod filets
- Salt and black pepper, to taste
- ½ cup flour
- 2 large eggs, beaten
- ½ teaspoon salt
- 1 cup Panko
- ½ cup grated parmesan
- 2 teaspoons old bay seasoning
- ½ teaspoon garlic powder
- Olive oil spray

Directions:
1. Rub the cod fillets with black pepper and salt.
2. Mix panko with parmesan cheese, old bay seasoning, and garlic powder in a bowl.
3. Mix flour with salt in another bowl.
4. Dredge the cod filets in the flour then dip in the eggs and coat with the Panko mixture.
5. Place the cod fillets in the air fryer baskets.
6. Return the air fryer basket 1 to Zone 1, and basket 2 to Zone 2 of the Ninja Foodi 2-Basket Air Fryer.
7. Choose the "Air Fry" mode for Zone 1 and set the temperature to 400 degrees F and 10 minutes of cooking time.
8. Select the "MATCH COOK" option to copy the settings for Zone 2.
9. Initiate cooking by pressing the START/PAUSE BUTTON.
10. Flip the cod fillets once cooked halfway through.
11. Serve warm.

Nutrition Info:
- (Per serving) Calories 275 | Fat 1.4g |Sodium 582mg | Carbs 31.5g | Fiber 1.1g | Sugar 0.1g | Protein 29.8g

Smoked Salmon

Servings:4
Cooking Time:12

Ingredients:
- 2 pounds of salmon fillets, smoked
- 6 ounces cream cheese
- 4 tablespoons mayonnaise
- 2 teaspoons of chives, fresh
- 1 teaspoon of lemon zest
- Salt and freshly ground black pepper, to taste
- 2 tablespoons of butter

Directions:
1. Cut the salmon into very small and uniform bite-size pieces.
2. Mix cream cheese, chives, mayonnaise, black pepper, and lemon zest, in a small mixing bowl.
3. Let it sit aside for further use.
4. Coat the salmon pieces with salt and butter.
5. Divide the bite-size pieces into both zones of the air fryer.
6. Set it on AIRFRY mode at 400 degrees F for 12 minutes.
7. Select MATCH for zone 2 basket.
8. Hit start, so the cooking start.
9. Once the salmon is done, top it with a bowl creamy mixture and serve.
10. Enjoy hot.

Nutrition Info:
- (Per serving) Calories 557| Fat 15.7 g| Sodium 371mg | Carbs 4.8 g | Fiber 0g | Sugar 1.1g | Protein 48 g

Two-way Salmon

Servings: 2
Cooking Time: 18

Ingredients:
- 2 salmon fillets, 8 ounces each
- 2 tablespoons of Cajun seasoning
- 2 tablespoons of jerk seasoning
- 1 lemon cut in half
- oil spray, for greasing

Directions:
1. First, drizzle lemon juice over the salmon and wash it with tap water.
2. Rinse and pat dry the fillets with a paper towel.
3. Now rub o fillet with Cajun seasoning and grease it with oil spray.
4. Take the second fillet and rub it with jerk seasoning.
5. Grease the second fillet of salmon with oil spray.
6. now put the salmon fillets in both the baskets.
7. Set the Zone 1 basket to 390 degrees F for 16-18 minutes
8. Select MATCH button for zone 2 basket.
9. hit the start button to start cooking.
10. Once the cooking is done, serve the fish hot with mayonnaise.

Nutrition Info:
- (Per serving) Calories 238| Fat 11.8g| Sodium 488mg | Carbs 9g | Fiber 0g | Sugar8 g | Protein 35g

Spicy Fish Fillet With Onion Rings

Servings: 1
Cooking Time: 12

Ingredients:
- 300 grams of onion rings, frozen and packed
- 1 codfish fillet, 8 ounces
- Salt and black pepper, to taste
- 1 teaspoon of lemon juice
- oil spray, for greasing

Directions:
1. Put the frozen onion rings in zone 1 basket of the air fryer.
2. Next pat dry the fish fillets with a paper towel and season them with salt, black pepper, and lemon juice.
3. Grease the fillet with oil spray.
4. Put the fish in zone 2 basket.
5. Use MAX crisp for zone 1 at 240 degrees for 9 minutes.
6. Use MAX crisp for zone 2 basket and set it to 210 degrees for 12 minutes.
7. Press sync and press start.
8. Once done, serve hot.

Nutrition Info:
- (Per serving) Calories 666| Fat23.5g| Sodium 911mg | Carbs 82g | Fiber 8.8g | Sugar 17.4g | Protein 30.4g

Salmon With Green Beans

Servings:1
Cooking Time:18

Ingredients:
- 1 salmon fillet, 2 inches thick
- 2 teaspoons of olive oil
- 2 teaspoons of smoked paprika
- Salt and black pepper, to taste
- 1 cup green beans
- Oil spray, for greasing

Directions:
1. Grease the green beans with oil spray and add them to zone 1 basket.
2. Now rub the salmon fillet with olive oil, smoked paprika, salt, and black pepper.
3. Put the salmon fillets in the zone 2 basket.
4. Now set the zone one basket to AIRFRY mode at 350 degrees F for 18 minutes.
5. Set the Zone 2 basket to 390 degrees F for 16-18 minutes
6. Hit the smart finish button.
7. Once done, take out the salmon and green beans and transfer them to the serving plates and enjoy.

Nutrition Info:
- (Per serving) Calories 367| Fat22 g| Sodium 87mg | Carbs 10.2g | Fiber 5.3g | Sugar 2g | Protein 37.2g

Codfish With Herb Vinaigrette

Servings:2
Cooking Time:16

Ingredients:
- Vinaigrette Ingredients:
- 1/2 cup parsley leaves
- 1 cup basil leaves
- ½ cup mint leaves
- 2 tablespoons thyme leaves
- 1/4 teaspoon red pepper flakes
- 2 cloves of garlic
- 4 tablespoons of red wine vinegar
- ¼ cup of olive oil
- Salt, to taste

- Other Ingredients:
- 1.5 pounds fish fillets, cod fish
- 2 tablespoons olive oil
- Salt and black pepper, to taste
- 1 teaspoon of paprika
- 1teasbpoon of Italian seasoning

Directions:
1. Blend the entire vinaigrette ingredient in a high-speed blender and pulse into a smooth paste.
2. Set aside for drizzling overcooked fish.
3. Rub the fillets with salt, black pepper, paprika, Italian seasoning, and olive oil.
4. Divide it between two baskets of the air fryer.
5. Set the zone 1 to 16 minutes at 390 degrees F, at AIR FRY mode.
6. Press the MATCH button for the second basket.
7. Once done, serve the fillets with the drizzle of blended vinaigrette

Nutrition Info:
- (Per serving) Calories 1219| Fat 81.8g| Sodium 1906mg | Carbs64.4 g | Fiber5.5 g | Sugar 0.4g | Protein 52.1g

Roasted Salmon And Parmesan Asparagus

Servings: 4
Cooking Time: 27 Minutes

Ingredients:
- 2 tablespoons Montreal steak seasoning
- 3 tablespoons brown sugar
- 3 uncooked salmon fillets (6 ounces each)
- 2 tablespoons canola oil, divided
- 1-pound asparagus, ends trimmed
- Kosher salt, as desired
- Ground black pepper, as desired
- ¼ cup shredded parmesan cheese, divided

Directions:
1. Combine the steak spice and brown sugar in a small bowl.
2. Brush 1 tablespoon of oil over the salmon fillets, then thoroughly coat with the sugar mixture.
3. Toss the asparagus with the remaining 1 tablespoon of oil, salt, and pepper in a mixing bowl.
4. Place a crisper plate in both drawers. Put the fillets skin-side down in the zone 1 drawer, then place the drawer in the unit. Insert the zone 2 drawer into the device after placing the asparagus in it.
5. Select zone 1, then ROAST, then set the temperature to 390 degrees F/ 200 degrees C with a 17-minute timer. To match the zone 2 settings to zone 1, choose MATCH. To begin cooking, press the START/STOP button.
6. When the zone 2 timer reaches 7 minutes, press START/STOP. Remove the zone 2 drawer from the unit. Flip the asparagus with silicone-tipped tongs. Re-insert the drawer into the unit. Continue cooking by pressing START/STOP.
7. When the zone 2 timer has reached 14 minutes, press START/STOP. Remove the zone 2 drawer from the unit. Sprinkle half the parmesan cheese over the asparagus, and mix lightly. Re-insert the drawer into the unit. Continue cooking by pressing START/STOP.
8. Transfer the fillets and asparagus to a serving plate once they've finished cooking. Serve with the remaining parmesan cheese on top of the asparagus.

Nutrition Info:
- (Per serving) Calories 293 | Fat 15.8g | Sodium 203mg | Carbs 11.1g | Fiber 2.4g | Sugar 8.7g | Protein 29g

Bang Bang Shrimp

Servings: 4
Cooking Time: 20 Minutes

Ingredients:
- For the shrimp:
- 1 cup corn starch
- Salt and pepper, to taste
- 2 pounds shrimp, peeled and deveined
- ½ to 1 cup buttermilk
- Cooking oil spray
- 1 large egg whisked with 1 teaspoon water
- For the sauce:
- 1/3 cup sweet Thai chili sauce
- ¼ cup sour cream
- ¼ cup mayonnaise
- 2 tablespoons buttermilk
- 1 tablespoon sriracha, or to taste
- Pinch dried dill weed

Directions:
1. Season the corn starch with salt and pepper in a wide, shallow bowl.
2. In a large mixing bowl, toss the shrimp in the buttermilk to coat them.
3. Dredge the shrimp in the seasoned corn starch.
4. Brush with the egg wash after spraying with cooking oil.
5. Place a crisper plate in each drawer. Place the shrimp in a single layer in each. You may need to cook in batches.
6. Select zone 1, then AIR FRY, then set the temperature to 360 degrees F/ 180 degrees C with a 5-minute timer. To match zone 2 settings to zone 1, choose MATCH. To begin, select START/STOP.
7. Meanwhile, combine all the sauce ingredients together in a bowl.
8. Remove the shrimp when the cooking time is over.

Nutrition Info:
- (Per serving) Calories 415 | Fat 15g | Sodium 1875mg | Carbs 28g | Fiber 1g | Sugar 5g | Protein 38g

Desserts Recipes

"air-fried" Oreos Apple Fries	62
Apple Crumble Peach Crumble	63
Banana Spring Rolls With Hot Fudge Dip	60
Brownie Muffins	58
Chocó Lava Cake	64
Chocolate Pudding	59
Dessert Empanadas	61
Fried Oreos	59
Healthy Semolina Pudding	64
Jelly Donuts	58
Mini Blueberry Pies	62
Pumpkin Muffins With Cinnamon	60
Strawberry Shortcake	63
Walnuts Fritters	61

Desserts Recipes

Jelly Donuts

Servings: 4
Cooking Time: 5 Minutes

Ingredients:
- 1 package Pillsbury Grands (Homestyle)
- ½ cup seedless raspberry jelly
- 1 tablespoon butter, melted
- ½ cup sugar

Directions:
1. Install a crisper plate in both drawers. Place half of the biscuits in the zone 1 drawer and half in zone 2's, then insert the drawers into the unit. You may need to cook in batches.
2. Select zone 1, select AIR FRY, set temperature to 390 degrees F/ 200 degrees C, and set time to 22 minutes. Select MATCH to match zone 2 settings to zone 1. Press the START/STOP button to begin cooking.
3. Place the sugar into a wide bowl with a flat bottom.
4. Baste all sides of the cooked biscuits with the melted butter and roll in the sugar to cover completely.
5. Using a long cake tip, pipe 1–2 tablespoons of raspberry jelly into each biscuit. You've now got raspberry-filled donuts!

Nutrition Info:
- (Per serving) Calories 252 | Fat 7g | Sodium 503mg | Carbs 45g | Fiber 0g | Sugar 23g | Protein 3g

Brownie Muffins

Servings: 10
Cooking Time: 15 Minutes

Ingredients:
- 2 eggs
- 96g all-purpose flour
- 1 tsp vanilla
- 130g powdered sugar
- 25g cocoa powder
- 37g pecans, chopped
- 1 tsp cinnamon
- 113g butter, melted

Directions:
1. In a bowl, whisk eggs, vanilla, butter, sugar, and cinnamon until well mixed.
2. Add cocoa powder and flour and stir until well combined.
3. Add pecans and fold well.
4. Pour batter into the silicone muffin moulds.
5. Insert a crisper plate in Ninja Foodi air fryer baskets.
6. Place muffin moulds in both baskets.
7. Select zone 1, then select "bake" mode and set the temperature to 360 degrees F for 15 minutes. Press "match" and then"start/stop" to begin.

Nutrition Info:
- (Per serving) Calories 210 | Fat 10.5g |Sodium 78mg | Carbs 28.7g | Fiber 1g | Sugar 20.2g | Protein 2.6g

Chocolate Pudding

Servings: 2
Cooking Time: 12 Minutes

Ingredients:
- 1 egg
- 32g all-purpose flour
- 35g cocoa powder
- 50g sugar
- 57g butter, melted
- ½ tsp baking powder

Directions:
1. In a bowl, mix flour, cocoa powder, sugar, and baking powder.
2. Add egg and butter and stir until well combined.
3. Pour batter into the two greased ramekins.
4. Insert a crisper plate in Ninja Foodi air fryer baskets.
5. Place ramekins in both baskets.
6. Select zone 1 then select "bake" mode and set the temperature to 375 degrees F for 12 minutes. Press match cook to match zone 2 settings to zone 1. Press "start/stop" to begin.

Nutrition Info:
- (Per serving) Calories 512 | Fat 27.3g | Sodium 198mg | Carbs 70.6g | Fiber 4.7g | Sugar 50.5g | Protein 7.2g

Fried Oreos

Servings: 8
Cooking Time: 8 Minutes

Ingredients:
- 1 can Pillsbury Crescent Dough (or equivalent)
- 8 Oreo cookies
- 1–2 tablespoons powdered sugar

Directions:
1. Open the crescent dough up and cut it into the right-size pieces to completely wrap each cookie.
2. Wrap each Oreo in dough. Make sure that there are no air bubbles and that the cookies are completely covered.
3. Install a crisper plate in both drawers. Place half the Oreo cookies in the zone 1 drawer and half in zone 2's. Sprinkle the tops with the powdered sugar, then insert the drawers into the unit.
4. Select zone 1, select AIR FRY, set temperature to 390 degrees F/ 200 degrees C, and set time to 8 minutes. Select MATCH to match zone 2 settings to zone 1. Press the START/STOP button to begin cooking.
5. Serve warm and enjoy!

Nutrition Info:
- (Per serving) Calories 338 | Fat 21.2g | Sodium 1503mg | Carbs 5.1g | Fiber 0.3g | Sugar 4.6g | Protein 29.3g

Banana Spring Rolls With Hot Fudge Dip

Servings:4
Cooking Time: 10 Minutes

Ingredients:
- FOR THE BANANA SPRING ROLLS
- 1 large banana
- 4 egg roll wrappers
- 4 teaspoons light brown sugar
- Nonstick cooking spray
- FOR THE HOT FUDGE DIP
- ¼ cup sweetened condensed milk
- 2 tablespoons semisweet chocolate chips
- 1 tablespoon unsweetened cocoa powder
- 1 tablespoon unsalted butter
- ⅛ teaspoon kosher salt
- ⅛ teaspoon vanilla extract

Directions:
1. To prep the banana spring rolls: Peel the banana and halve it crosswise. Cut each piece in half lengthwise, for a total of 4 pieces.
2. Place one piece of banana diagonally across an egg roll wrapper. Sprinkle with 1 teaspoon of brown sugar. Fold the edges of the egg roll wrapper over the ends of the banana, then roll to enclose the banana inside. Brush the edge of the wrapper with water and press to seal. Spritz with cooking spray. Repeat with the remaining bananas, egg roll wrappers, and brown sugar.
3. To prep the hot fudge dip: In an ovenproof ramekin or bowl, combine the condensed milk, chocolate chips, cocoa powder, butter, salt, and vanilla.
4. To cook the spring rolls and hot fudge dip: Install a crisper plate in each of the two baskets. Place the banana spring rolls seam-side down in the Zone 1 basket and insert the basket in the unit. Place the ramekin in the Zone 2 basket and insert the basket in the unit.
5. Select Zone 1, select AIR FRY, set the temperature to 390°F, and set the timer to 10 minutes.
6. Select Zone 2, select BAKE, set the temperature to 330°F, and set the timer to 8 minutes. Select SMART FINISH.
7. Press START/PAUSE to begin cooking.
8. When the Zone 2 timer reads 3 minutes, press START/PAUSE. Remove the basket and stir the hot fudge until smooth. Reinsert the basket and press START/PAUSE to resume cooking.
9. When cooking is complete, the spring rolls should be crisp.
10. Let the hot fudge cool for 2 to 3 minutes. Serve the banana spring rolls with hot fudge for dipping.

Nutrition Info:
- (Per serving) Calories: 268; Total fat: 10g; Saturated fat: 4g; Carbohydrates: 42g; Fiber: 2g; Protein: 5g; Sodium: 245mg

Pumpkin Muffins With Cinnamon

Servings: 4
Cooking Time: 20 Minutes

Ingredients:
- 1 and ½ cups all-purpose flour
- ½ teaspoon baking soda
- ½ teaspoon baking powder
- 1 and ¼ teaspoons cinnamon, groaned
- ¼ teaspoon ground nutmeg, grated
- 2 large eggs
- Salt, pinch
- ¾ cup granulated sugar
- ½ cup dark brown sugar
- 1 and ½ cups pumpkin puree
- ¼ cup coconut milk

Directions:
1. Take 4 ramekins and layer them with muffin paper.
2. In a bowl, add the eggs, brown sugar, baking soda, baking powder, cinnamon, nutmeg, and sugar and whisk well with an electric mixer.
3. In a second bowl, mix the flour, and salt.
4. Slowly add the dry ingredients to the wet ingredients.
5. Fold in the pumpkin puree and milk and mix it in well.
6. Divide this batter into 4 ramekins.
7. Place two ramekins in each air fryer basket.
8. Set the time for zone 1 to 18 minutes at 360 degrees F/ 180 degrees C on AIR FRY mode.
9. Select the MATCH button for the zone 2 basket.
10. Check after the time is up and if not done, and let it AIR FRY for one more minute.
11. Once it is done, serve.

Nutrition Info:
- (Per serving) Calories 291 | Fat 6.4g | Sodium 241mg | Carbs 57.1g | Fiber 4.4g | Sugar 42g | Protein 5.9g

Walnuts Fritters

Servings: 6
Cooking Time: 15 Minutes.

Ingredients:
- 1 cup all-purpose flour
- ½ cup walnuts, chopped
- ¼ cup white sugar
- ¼ cup milk
- 1 egg
- 1 ½ teaspoons baking powder
- 1 pinch salt
- Cooking spray
- 2 tablespoons white sugar
- ½ teaspoon ground cinnamon
- Glaze:
- ½ cup confectioners› sugar
- 1 tablespoon milk
- ½ teaspoon caramel extract
- ¼ teaspoons ground cinnamon

Directions:
1. Layer both crisper plate with parchment paper.
2. Grease the parchment paper with cooking spray.
3. Whisk flour with milk, ¼ cup of sugar, egg, baking powder, and salt in a small bowl.
4. Separately mix 2 tablespoons of sugar with cinnamon in another bowl, toss in walnuts and mix well to coat.
5. Stir in flour mixture and mix until combined.
6. Drop the fritters mixture using a cookie scoop into the two crisper plate.
7. Return the crisper plate to the Ninja Foodi Dual Zone Air Fryer.
8. Choose the Air Fry mode for Zone 1 and set the temperature to 375 degrees F and the time to 15 minutes.
9. Select the "MATCH" button to copy the settings for Zone 2.
10. Initiate cooking by pressing the START/STOP button.
11. Flip the fritters once cooked halfway through, then resume cooking.
12. Meanwhile, whisk milk, caramel extract, confectioners' sugar, and cinnamon in a bowl.
13. Transfer fritters to a wire rack and allow them to cool.
14. Drizzle with a glaze over the fritters.

Nutrition Info:
- (Per serving) Calories 391 | Fat 24g |Sodium 142mg | Carbs 38.5g | Fiber 3.5g | Sugar 21g | Protein 6.6g

Dessert Empanadas

Servings: 12
Cooking Time: 10 Minutes

Ingredients:
- 12 empanada wrappers thawed
- 2 apples, chopped
- 2 tablespoons raw honey
- 1 teaspoon vanilla extract
- 1 teaspoon cinnamon
- ⅛ teaspoon nutmeg
- 2 teaspoons cornstarch
- 1 teaspoon water
- 1 egg beaten

Directions:
1. Mix apples with vanilla, honey, nutmeg, and cinnamon in a saucepan.
2. Cook for 3 minutes then mix cornstarch with water and pour into the pan.
3. Cook for 30 seconds.
4. Allow this filling to cool and keep it aside.
5. Spread the wrappers on the working surface.
6. Divide the apple filling on top of the wrappers.
7. Fold the wrappers in half and seal the edges by pressing them.
8. Brush the empanadas with the beaten egg and place them in the air fryer basket 1.
9. Return the air fryer basket 1 to Zone 1 of the Ninja Foodi 2-Basket Air Fryer.
10. Choose the "Air Fry" mode for Zone 1 at 400 degrees F and 10 minutes of cooking time.
11. Initiate cooking by pressing the START/PAUSE BUTTON.
12. Flip the empanadas once cooked halfway through.
13. Serve.

Nutrition Info:
- (Per serving) Calories 204 | Fat 9g |Sodium 91mg | Carbs 27g | Fiber 2.4g | Sugar 15g | Protein 1.3g

"air-fried" Oreos Apple Fries

Servings: 4
Cooking Time: 10 Minutes

Ingredients:
- FOR THE "FRIED" OREOS
- 1 teaspoon vegetable oil
- 1 cup all-purpose flour
- 1 tablespoon granulated sugar
- 1 tablespoon baking powder
- ½ teaspoon baking soda
- ¼ teaspoon kosher salt
- 1 large egg
- ¼ cup unsweetened almond milk
- ½ teaspoon vanilla extract
- 8 Oreo cookies
- Nonstick cooking spray
- 1 tablespoon powdered sugar (optional)
- FOR THE APPLE FRIES
- 1 teaspoon vegetable oil
- 1 cup all-purpose flour
- 1 tablespoon granulated sugar
- 1 tablespoon baking powder
- ½ teaspoon baking soda
- ¼ teaspoon kosher salt
- 1 large egg
- ¼ cup unsweetened almond milk
- ½ teaspoon vanilla extract
- 2 Granny Smith apples
- 2 tablespoons cornstarch
- ½ teaspoon apple pie spice
- Nonstick cooking spray
- 1 tablespoon powdered sugar (optional)

Directions:
1. To prep the "fried" Oreos: Brush a crisper plate with the oil and install it in the Zone 1 basket.
2. In a large bowl, combine the flour, granulated sugar, baking powder, baking soda, and salt. Mix in the egg, almond milk, and vanilla to form a thick batter.
3. Using a fork or slotted spoon, dip each cookie into the batter, coating it fully. Let the excess batter drip off, then place the cookies in the prepared basket in a single layer. Spritz each with cooking spray.
4. To prep the apple fries: Brush a crisper plate with the oil and install it in the Zone 2 basket.
5. In a large bowl, combine the flour, granulated sugar, baking powder, baking soda, and salt. Mix in the egg, almond milk, and vanilla to form a thick batter.
6. Core the apples and cut them into ½-inch-thick French fry shapes. Dust lightly with the cornstarch and apple pie spice.
7. Using a fork or slotted spoon, dip each apple into the batter, coating it fully. Let the excess batter drip off, then place the apples in the prepared basket in a single layer. Spritz with cooking spray.
8. To cook the "fried" Oreos and apple fries: Insert both baskets in the unit.
9. Select Zone 1, select AIR FRY, set the temperature to 400°F, and set the timer to 8 minutes.
10. Select Zone 2, select AIR FRY, set the temperature to 400°F, and set the timer to 10 minutes. Select SMART FINISH.
11. Press START/PAUSE to begin cooking.
12. When cooking is complete, the batter will be golden brown and crisp. If desired, dust the cookies and apples with the powdered sugar before serving.

Nutrition Info:
- (Per serving) Calories: 464; Total fat: 21g; Saturated fat: 3.5g; Carbohydrates: 66g; Fiber: 2.5g; Protein: 7g; Sodium: 293mg

Mini Blueberry Pies

Servings: 2
Cooking Time: 10

Ingredients:
- 1 box Store-Bought Pie Dough, Trader Joe's
- ¼ cup blueberry jam
- 1 teaspoon of lemon zest
- 1 egg white, for brushing

Directions:
1. Take the store brought pie dough and cut it into 3-inch circles.
2. Brush the dough with egg white all around the parameters.
3. Now add blueberry jam and zest in the middle and top it with another circular.
4. Press the edges with the fork to seal it.
5. Make a slit in the middle of the dough and divide it between the baskets.
6. Set zone 1 to AIR FRY mode 360 degrees for 10 minutes.
7. Select the MATCH button for zone 2.
8. Once cooked, serve.

Nutrition Info:
- (Per serving) Calories 234| Fat 8.6g| Sodium 187 mg | Carbs 38.2 g | Fiber 0.1g | Sugar 13.7 g | Protein 2g

Strawberry Shortcake

Servings: 8
Cooking Time: 9 Minutes

Ingredients:
- Strawberry topping
- 1-pint strawberries sliced
- ½ cup confectioner's sugar substitute
- Shortcake
- 2 cups Carbquick baking biscuit mix
- ¼ cup butter cold, cubed
- ½ cup confectioner's sugar substitute
- Pinch salt
- ⅔ cup water
- Garnish: sugar free whipped cream

Directions:
1. Mix the shortcake ingredients in a bowl until smooth.
2. Divide the dough into 6 biscuits.
3. Place the biscuits in the air fryer basket 1.
4. Return the air fryer basket 1 to Zone 1 of the Ninja Foodi 2-Basket Air Fryer.
5. Choose the "Air Fry" mode for Zone 1 and set the temperature 400 degrees F and 9 minutes of cooking time.
6. Initiate cooking by pressing the START/PAUSE BUTTON.
7. Mix strawberries with sugar in a saucepan and cook until the mixture thickens.
8. Slice the biscuits in half and add strawberry sauce in between two halves of a biscuit.
9. Serve.

Nutrition Info:
- (Per serving) Calories 157 | Fat 1.3g |Sodium 27mg | Carbs 1.3g | Fiber 1g | Sugar 2.2g | Protein 8.2g

Apple Crumble Peach Crumble

Servings: 8
Cooking Time: 20 Minutes

Ingredients:
- FOR THE APPLE CRUMBLE
- ½ cup packed light brown sugar
- ¼ cup all-purpose flour
- ¼ cup rolled oats
- 2 tablespoons unsalted butter, at room temperature
- ½ teaspoon ground cinnamon
- ¼ teaspoon ground nutmeg
- ⅛ teaspoon kosher salt
- 4 medium Granny Smith apples, sliced
- FOR THE PEACH CRUMBLE
- ½ cup packed light brown sugar
- ¼ cup all-purpose flour
- ¼ cup rolled oats
- 2 tablespoons unsalted butter, at room temperature
- ½ teaspoon ground cinnamon
- ⅛ teaspoon kosher salt
- 4 peaches, peeled and sliced

Directions:
1. To prep the apple crumble: In a medium bowl, combine the brown sugar, flour, oats, butter, cinnamon, nutmeg, and salt and mix well. The mixture will be dry and crumbly.
2. To prep the peach crumble: In a medium bowl, combine the brown sugar, flour, oats, butter, cinnamon, and salt and mix well. The mixture will be dry and crumbly.
3. To cook both crumbles: Spread the apples in the Zone 1 basket in an even layer. Top evenly with the apple crumble topping and insert the basket in the unit. Spread the peaches in the Zone 2 basket in an even layer. Top with the peach crumble topping and insert the basket in the unit.
4. Select Zone 1, select BAKE, set the temperature to 350°F, and set the timer to 20 minutes. Select MATCH COOK to match Zone 2 settings to Zone 1.
5. Press START/PAUSE to begin cooking.
6. When cooking is complete, the fruit will be tender and the crumble topping crisp and golden brown. Serve warm or at room temperature.

Nutrition Info:
- (Per serving) Calories: 300; Total fat: 6.5g; Saturated fat: 3.5g; Carbohydrates: 59g; Fiber: 5.5g; Protein: 2g; Sodium: 45mg

Ninja Dual Zone Air Fryer Cookbook

Chocó Lava Cake

Servings: 4
Cooking Time: 10 Minutes

Ingredients:
- 3 eggs
- 3 egg yolks
- 70g dark chocolate, chopped
- 168g cups powdered sugar
- 96g all-purpose flour
- 1 tsp vanilla
- 113g butter
- ½ tsp salt

Directions:
1. Add chocolate and butter to a bowl and microwave for 30 seconds. Remove from oven and stir until smooth.
2. Add eggs, egg yolks, sugar, flour, vanilla, and salt into the melted chocolate and stir until well combined.
3. Pour batter into the four greased ramekins.
4. Insert a crisper plate in Ninja Foodi air fryer baskets.
5. Place ramekins in both baskets.
6. Select zone 1 then select "air fry" mode and set the temperature to 390 degrees F for 10 minutes. Press "match" to match zone 2 settings to zone 1. Press "start/stop" to begin.

Nutrition Info:
- (Per serving) Calories 687 | Fat 37.3g |Sodium 527mg | Carbs 78.3g | Fiber 1.5g | Sugar 57.4g | Protein 10.7g

Healthy Semolina Pudding

Servings: 4
Cooking Time: 20 Minutes

Ingredients:
- 45g semolina
- 1 tsp vanilla
- 500ml milk
- 115g caster sugar

Directions:
1. Mix semolina and ½ cup milk in a bowl. Slowly add the remaining milk, sugar, and vanilla and mix well.
2. Pour the mixture into four greased ramekins.
3. Insert a crisper plate in the Ninja Foodi air fryer baskets.
4. Place ramekins in both baskets.
5. Select zone 1, then select "air fry" mode and set the temperature to 300 degrees F for 20 minutes. Press "match" to match zone 2 settings to zone 1. Press "start/stop" to begin.

Nutrition Info:
- (Per serving) Calories 209 | Fat 2.7g |Sodium 58mg | Carbs 41.5g | Fiber 0.6g | Sugar 30.6g | Protein 5.8g

RECIPES

DATE

RECIPES	Salads	Meats	Soups
SERVES	Grains	Seafood	Snack
PREP TIME	Breads	Vegetables	Breakfast
COOK TIME	Appetizers	Desserts	Lunch
FROM THE KITCHEN OF	Main Dishes	Beverages	Dinners

INGREDIENTS

_____
_____
_____
_____
_____

DIRECTIONS

_____
_____
_____
_____
_____
_____
_____
_____

NOTES

SERVING ☆☆☆☆☆

DIFFICULTY ☆☆☆☆☆

OVERALL ☆☆☆☆☆

Ninja Dual Zone Air Fryer Cookbook

How to Reduce Food Waste

- Plan Meals: Create a weekly meal plan and shopping list.

- Store Food Properly: Use airtight containers and maintain the right temperature.

- FIFO Rule: Consume older items before newer ones.

- Portion Control: Serve smaller portions to avoid leftovers.

- Use Leftovers: Repurpose or freeze them.

- Understand Expiry Dates: Many foods are safe past these dates.

- Composting: Start a compost bin for food scraps.

- Donate: Share surplus non-perishables with food banks.

- Shop Mindfully: Buy in bulk, choose minimal packaging.

- Batch Cooking: Prep and freeze meals for later.

- Preserve Foods: Learn canning, pickling, and drying.

- Spread Awareness: Educate and inspire others.

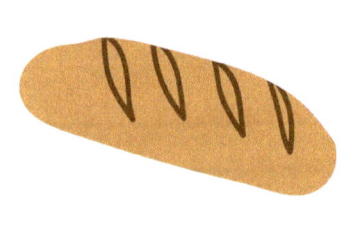

Date: _____

MY SHOPPING LIST

Appendix A : Measurement Conversions

BASIC KITCHEN CONVERSIONS & EQUIVALENTS

DRY MEASUREMENTS CONVERSION CHART

3 TEASPOONS = 1 TABLESPOON = 1/16 CUP

6 TEASPOONS = 2 TABLESPOONS = 1/8 CUP

12 TEASPOONS = 4 TABLESPOONS = 1/4 CUP

24 TEASPOONS = 8 TABLESPOONS = 1/2 CUP

36 TEASPOONS = 12 TABLESPOONS = 3/4 CUP

48 TEASPOONS = 16 TABLESPOONS = 1 CUP

METRIC TO US COOKING CONVERSIONS

OVEN TEMPERATURES

120 °C = 250 °F

160 °C = 320 °F

180° C = 350 °F

205 °C = 400 °F

220 °C = 425 °F

LIQUID MEASUREMENTS CONVERSION CHART

8 FLUID OUNCES = 1 CUP = 1/2 PINT = 1/4 QUART

16 FLUID OUNCES = 2 CUPS = 1 PINT = 1/2 QUART

32 FLUID OUNCES = 4 CUPS = 2 PINTS = 1 QUART = 1/4 GALLON

128 FLUID OUNCES = 16 CUPS = 8 PINTS = 4 QUARTS = 1 GALLON

BAKING IN GRAMS

1 CUP FLOUR = 140 GRAMS

1 CUP SUGAR = 150 GRAMS

1 CUP POWDERED SUGAR = 160 GRAMS

1 CUP HEAVY CREAM = 235 GRAMS

VOLUME

1 MILLILITER = 1/5 TEASPOON

5 ML = 1 TEASPOON

15 ML = 1 TABLESPOON

240 ML = 1 CUP OR 8 FLUID OUNCES

1 LITER = 34 FL. OUNCES

WEIGHT

1 GRAM = .035 OUNCES

100 GRAMS = 3.5 OUNCES

500 GRAMS = 1.1 POUNDS

1 KILOGRAM = 35 OUNCES

US TO METRIC COOKING CONVERSIONS

1/5 TSP = 1 ML

1 TSP = 5 ML

1 TBSP = 15 ML

1 FL OUNCE = 30 ML

1 CUP = 237 ML

1 PINT (2 CUPS) = 473 ML

1 QUART (4 CUPS) = .95 LITER

1 GALLON (16 CUPS) = 3.8 LITERS

1 OZ = 28 GRAMS

1 POUND = 454 GRAMS

BUTTER

1 CUP BUTTER = 2 STICKS = 8 OUNCES = 230 GRAMS = 8 TABLESPOONS

WHAT DOES 1 CUP EQUAL

1 CUP = 8 FLUID OUNCES

1 CUP = 16 TABLESPOONS

1 CUP = 48 TEASPOONS

1 CUP = 1/2 PINT

1 CUP = 1/4 QUART

1 CUP = 1/16 GALLON

1 CUP = 240 ML

BAKING PAN CONVERSIONS

1 CUP ALL-PURPOSE FLOUR = 4.5 OZ

1 CUP ROLLED OATS = 3 OZ 1 LARGE EGG = 1.7 OZ

1 CUP BUTTER = 8 OZ 1 CUP MILK = 8 OZ

1 CUP HEAVY CREAM = 8.4 OZ

1 CUP GRANULATED SUGAR = 7.1 OZ

1 CUP PACKED BROWN SUGAR = 7.75 OZ

1 CUP VEGETABLE OIL = 7.7 OZ

1 CUP UNSIFTED POWDERED SUGAR = 4.4 OZ

BAKING PAN CONVERSIONS

9-INCH ROUND CAKE PAN = 12 CUPS

10-INCH TUBE PAN = 16 CUPS

11-INCH BUNDT PAN = 12 CUPS

9-INCH SPRINGFORM PAN = 10 CUPS

9 X 5 INCH LOAF PAN = 8 CUPS

9-INCH SQUARE PAN = 8 CUPS

Appendix B : Recipes index

A

Acorn Squash Slices   27
Air Fried Lamb Chops   37
Air Fried Okra   29
Air Fryer Vegetables   31

"air-fried" Oreos Apple Fries   62
Almond Chicken   47
Apple Crumble Peach Crumble   63
Asian Pork Skewers   33

B

Bacon Wrapped Tater Tots   18
Bacon-wrapped Chicken   44
Banana Spring Rolls With Hot Fudge Dip   60
Bang Bang Shrimp   56
Beef & Broccoli   38
Beef Jerky Pineapple Jerky   20

Beets With Orange Gremolata And Goat's Cheese   30
Biscuit Balls   13
Breakfast Casserole   12
Breakfast Cheese Sandwich   8
Breakfast Stuffed Peppers   10
Brownie Muffins   58

C

Cauliflower Gnocchi   19
Chicken Cordon Bleu   45
Chili Chicken Wings   46
Chili Lime Tilapia   51
Chocó Lava Cake   64
Chocolate Pudding   59
Cinnamon Apple French Toast   13

Cinnamon-apple Pork Chops   34
Cinnamon-raisin Bagels Everything Bagels   11
Codfish With Herb Vinaigrette   55
Cornish Hen With Asparagus   45
Crispy Hash Browns   9
Crispy Parmesan Cod   53
Crispy Tortilla Chips   22

D

Delicious Chicken Skewers   42
Delicious Haddock   52
Dessert Empanadas   61

Dijon Chicken Wings   43
Donuts   8

F

Fried Lobster Tails   51
Fried Oreos   59

"fried" Fish With Seasoned Potato Wedges   52

G

Garlic Bread 18
Garlic Herbed Baked Potatoes 25
Garlic Potato Wedges In Air Fryer 29
Garlic-herb Fried Squash 30
Garlic-rosemary Brussels Sprouts 26
Garlic, Buffalo, And Blue Cheese Stuffed Chicken 44
Glazed Thighs With French Fries 46

H

Healthy Oatmeal Muffins 12
Healthy Semolina Pudding 64
Herb And Lemon Cauliflower 25
Honey Banana Oatmeal 11
Honey Butter Chicken 43

I

Italian Chicken & Potatoes 42
Italian-style Meatballs With Garlicky Roasted Broccoli 36

J

Jelly Donuts 58
Jerk Tofu With Roasted Cabbage 27
Juicy Pork Chops 39

K

Korean Bbq Beef 39

L

Lamb Chops With Dijon Garlic 37
Lamb Shank With Mushroom Sauce 34

M

Meatloaf 36
Mexican Jalapeno Poppers 22
Mini Blueberry Pies 62
Mozzarella Sticks 23
Mustard Rubbed Lamb Chops 35

O

Onion Rings 23

P

Parmesan Crush Chicken 21
Parmesan Pork Chops 33
Pepper Poppers 26
Peppered Asparagus 17
Pork Tenderloin With Brown Sugar–pecan Sweet

Potatoes 35
Potato Tater Tots 19
Potatoes & Beans 28
Pumpkin Muffins With Cinnamon 60

R

Ravioli 17

Roasted Salmon And Parmesan Asparagus 56

S

Salmon With Green Beans 55
Sausage & Butternut Squash 9
Scallops With Greens 50
Smoked Salmon 53
Spanakopita Rolls With Mediterranean Vegetable Salad 28
Spicy Fish Fillet With Onion Rings 54

Spicy Salmon Fillets 50
Spinach And Red Pepper Egg Cups With Coffee-glazed Canadian Bacon 10
Steak And Mashed Creamy Potatoes 38
Strawberry Shortcake 63
Stuffed Bell Peppers 21

T

Thai Chicken Meatballs 48
Tofu Veggie Meatballs 20

Turkey Meatloaf With Veggie Medley 48
Two-way Salmon 54

V

Vanilla Strawberry Doughnuts 14

Veggie Stuffed Chicken Breasts 47

W

Walnuts Fritters 61

Y

Yellow Potatoes With Eggs 14

Z

Zucchini With Stuffing 31

Printed in Great Britain
by Amazon